D0707909

C153920774

Supper for a Song

Supper
for a Song

Tamasin Day-Lewis

Quadrille
PUBLISHING

Photography by JAMES MERRELL

Notes • Use fresh herbs, sea salt and freshly ground black pepper unless otherwise suggested. • Use large eggs, organic or at least free-range. Anyone who is pregnant or in a vulnerable health group should avoid recipes that use raw egg whites or lightly cooked eggs. • Timings are for conventional ovens. If using a fan-assisted oven, reduce the temperature by 15°C (1 Gas mark). Use an oven thermometer to check the temperature. • Both metric and imperial measures are given for the recipes. Follow one set or the other, not a combination of the two, as they are not interchangeable.

How to cook a chicken...

This is not meant to be an insult, after all, you all know how to cook a chicken, but maybe you're not so good at making the bird pay full fare.

You've had your Sunday roast, cleared up the greasy roasting tins, snaffled a final roastie and the last thing you feel like doing is getting the stockpot going. You put the bare bones, carefully wrapped, in the fridge for tomorrow or the next day, or next week, when you'll find them there staring you out accusingly and chuck them away. But you somehow can't quite bring yourself to throw them away now.

Or, you've given everyone giant second helpings, not wanting to be mean, not wanting to say you would really like to keep a leg and a breast aside for supper the next day. You will have to start cooking from scratch again tomorrow. It will cost time and money, which is infuriating when you could have been halfway there – only needing to raid the fridge and your imagination to come up with Chicken Reincarnation.

I'm sure you have all wished you had been just that bit more think-aheaded about things. And that having thought ahead you would be all set to spice up those errant wings you clipped before the bird got trussed and roasted, and slow-cook them in a brew of lime and ginger, garlic and molasses, chilli and more chilli, and dunk them into a blue cheese dressing.

If only you hadn't stripped the meat from your roast as close as a No 1 haircut down to the carcass and ripped every last scrap

again and again

from its undercarriage until there wasn't a pick of flesh left on it.
If you had stretched the bird as far as it would go, likewise the
sausage, there would be a heap of extra stuffing, porky and pruney
and thick with onion and sage, to deliver to your table on a dull,
dreary Monday night in the shape of a magnificent sausage pie
with a golden crust. All for so much less effort than if you'd had to
start from scratch. And you would still have stock for a soup, and
other juicy morsels to plop into a creamy, lemon chicken risotto,
where the meat is really not centre stage – it is a walk-on part.

When I'm creating something out of nothing, or turning the old
into new, I really feel I am cooking. You could say it is hard-times
cookery, 'willful waste makes woeful want' and all that, but it is
so satisfying, that ultimately, it is less about the scrimping and
saving and putting a secondhand rose on the plate than it is about
showing you are a creative cook and can work with whatever
you've got to hand.

What do we throw away most? Chicken carcasses, lettuce
leaves and limp vegetables, scraps of cheese and stale bread,
chick peas that we've cooked too many of, and old, cold potatoes.
The list is as long as your shopping list.

There is a wonderful expression about how when eating a pig
you should eat everything but the squeak. That is what this
chapter is about, and here are some ways you can do it and feel
proud of yourself, proud that you used every little last bit up and
what you made was never less than a supper that made you sing.

Roast chicken
with sausage, sage and prune stuffing

The point of buying a larger-than-you-need chicken is that you then have another crack of the whip. Roast a generously stuffed, good-sized chicken and serve it with lots of different vegetables, including roast potatoes and parsnips, and you really don't need to offer large helpings of meat. There will be plenty left over to make a risotto, pie or salad. You can also double the amount of stuffing to give you enough to make a sausage pie for supper the following evening (see page 13). If you do not have sage, prunes work well with thyme too.

serves 6 (in its first incarnation)

1 organic or at least free-range chicken, about 2–2.5kg/4½–5½lb (giblets saved for gravy)

1 large onion, peeled and sliced

a little olive oil

sea salt and black pepper

for the stuffing

450–500g/1–1lb 2oz packet good plain pork sausages

2 tbsp olive oil

a walnut-sized knob of butter

1 red onion, peeled and finely chopped

2 celery stalks, de-strung with a potato peeler and finely chopped with the leaves

about 12 sage leaves, finely chopped

about 18 prunes, preferably Agen, pitted and roughly chopped

2 slices stale bread, crusts removed and blitzed to crumbs

finely grated zest of 2 organic oranges

1 organic large egg, beaten

for the gravy

glass of red wine

vegetable cooking water (ideally from parboiling potatoes and parsnips)

Preheat the oven to 200°C/Gas 6. Have the chicken ready at room temperature. Put the sliced onion in the bottom of your roasting tin.

For the stuffing, slit the sausage skins and tip the meat into a large bowl; set aside. Heat the olive oil and butter in a heavy-bottomed frying pan and add the onion, celery and chopped sage. Cook over a medium-low heat until the vegetables have begun to soften and turn translucent. Throw in the prunes and remove from the heat a couple of minutes later; do not stir them around too much as you don't want them to turn mushy. Let cool slightly, then add to the sausage meat with the breadcrumbs and orange zest. Season lightly, as the sausages will be seasoned already. Now add the beaten egg and gently turn the mixture until it coheres.

Stuff the chicken and secure the opening. Stand the bird on the sliced onion in the roasting tin, douse with a little olive oil, season and put into the oven to roast. A bird this size should take between 1 hour 20 minutes and 1 hour 40 minutes, by which time the skin will have crisped and turned bronze. Add the giblets to the roasting tin for the last 20 minutes. To test if it is cooked, insert a skewer into the thickest part of the thigh. If the juices run clear, not bloody, the bird is cooked.

Transfer the bird to a warm platter and leave to rest, covered loosely with foil, in a warm place for 10–15 minutes while you make the gravy and finish off the accompanying vegetables before carving. For the gravy, pour off any excess fat from the roasting tin, then set it over a medium-high heat. Add the wine and stir with a wooden spoon to deglaze, crushing the chicken liver as you do so. Let bubble for a minute or two, then add the cooking water and let bubble to reduce and thicken to the desired consistency. Press through a sieve into a warm serving jug.

Slice the breast thinly and give everyone a few slices and either a wing or a third of a leg, depending on appetite and how much meat you would like left over. Give everyone a generous helping of stuffing. Pour all the juices from the carving board into the gravy. Remove the bird from sight!

Cover the remains of the bird once it has cooled but do not pick the meat at this stage unless you are going to make stock immediately, as it dries much more quickly off the carcass.

Spicy chicken wings
with blue cheese dressing

I am convinced it's a male conspiracy that girls are supposed to like the light meat and boys the dark, as the best flavoured meat on a chicken is the dark. After all, what the men carve for themselves must be the best. And there are so many people who don't make the best use of every little nook and cranny of their chook. Why do we cut the feet off? The French don't, nor do the Chinese, they know that ten toes add a lovely glueyness to stocks and soups in the same way as the addition of a pig's trotter does.

At the Taunton farmers' market on a Thursday, Jason of The Ark Chicken Company is only too pleased that there are a few of us not just demanding chicken breasts. He sells wings by the bag and they are the most delectable of things to get your tongue round and suck and pick right down to the bone. Add a spicy sauce and you have a starter that doesn't look amiss at a good dinner, the cost bearing no relation to the sumptuousness of the taste.

Start this recipe the night before so the bones have time to marinate.

serves 4 as a starter

12–16 chicken wings

for the marinade

2 tsp toasted sesame oil

1 heaped tbsp black treacle or blackstrap molasses

1 heaped tbsp golden syrup

2 tbsp tomato ketchup

juice of 1 lime

1 thumb fresh root ginger, peeled and grated

2 garlic cloves, peeled and crushed

1 red chilli, deseeded and very finely chopped, or 1 dried chilli, crumbled, or 1 tsp chilli flakes, or cayenne pepper to taste

for the dressing

3 tbsp soured cream

6 tbsp home-made mayonnaise

2 tsp Worcestershire sauce

¼ tsp crushed garlic

sea salt and black pepper

85g/3oz blue cheese, such as Beenleigh, Cashel, Stilton or Stichelton, crumbled

Mix all the marinade ingredients together and taste – you may want to adjust the quantities depending on your heat and sharp and spice taste. Throw the chicken wings into a large Ziplock bag and pour in the marinade. Seal the bag, squelch around a bit and leave to marinate overnight in the fridge.

For the blue cheese dressing, whisk the soured cream, mayonnaise, Worcestershire sauce and garlic together in a bowl with some seasoning, remembering that the cheese will be salty. Fold in the crumbled cheese, check the seasoning, cover and chill until you need it.

Bring the chicken wings to room temperature before you cook them. Preheat the oven to 140°C/Gas 1. Line a baking tray, large enough to hold all the wings in a single layer, with foil. Tip the wings onto the tray and pour over the marinade. Cook for about 2 hours, turning them over from time to time to ensure the sauce doesn't dry out.

Serve the chicken wings hot on a platter with the chilled blue cheese dressing, so that everyone can help themselves and dip the wings into the dressing.

Lemon chicken risotto

A little chicken goes a long way in this dish, which is an adaptation of my favourite Italian food writer Anna Del Conte's recipe. It has the soothing quality a proper risotto should have, with its almost chalky-textured rice that combines bite and firmness with sloppiness.

I normally use the king of risotto rice, carnaroli, for this dish, but Arborio or vialone nano might suit your budget better.

serves 4

1 tbsp olive oil

55g/2oz unsalted butter

2 shallots, peeled and very finely chopped

1 celery stalk, de-strung with a potato peeler and finely chopped

285g/10oz risotto rice

1 litre/1¾ pints vegetable or chicken stock

6 sage leaves, rolled up and shredded

1 small sprig of rosemary, needles chopped

finely grated zest and juice of 1 organic lemon

1 organic large egg yolk

4 tbsp freshly grated Parmesan, plus extra to serve

4 tbsp double cream

sea salt and black pepper

140–180g/5–6oz cooked dark and white chicken meat, diced

Heat the olive oil with half of the butter in a heavy-bottomed medium saucepan and add the shallots and celery. Cook gently, stirring occasionally, for about 7 minutes until softened (this is a *soffrito*). Tip in the risotto rice and stir to coat for a couple of minutes.

Heat the stock and keep it at simmering point throughout the cooking. Pour about 150ml/¼ pint onto the rice and stir vigorously until most of it has been absorbed, before adding some more and stirring again until absorbed. Continue in this way, adding the chopped mixed herbs and lemon zest roughly halfway through cooking, which takes about 20–22 minutes altogether.

In a small bowl, combine the egg yolk, the juice of ½ lemon, the Parmesan and the cream, then scrunch over some black pepper generously. Mix well with a fork.

When the rice is cooked but still al dente, take the pan from the heat and stir in the egg and cream mixture, cooked chicken and remaining butter. Add another ladleful of hot stock.

Cover the pan and leave to rest for 5 minutes off the heat. Check the seasoning and adjust if necessary, adding more lemon juice if you think it is needed. Give the pan a short stir and serve at once, with extra Parmesan passed around in a bowl.

You can omit the cooked chicken from the recipe if you like and just serve the risotto on its own with a green salad to follow. Or for a traditional Milanese dish, sauté some chicken joints in butter to colour, then cook them in a casserole in the oven with 200ml/7fl oz double cream and serve the lemon risotto as an accompaniment.

Sausage pie

This is real food, outdoors food fit for a late summer picnic, a shoot lunch or a cold day's walk. Good sausage meat, spicing and pastry, it is comforting stuff, made a little lighter and more elegant by having no top deck and only the best ingredients. Fine, too, for the Atlantic Irish breezes on a west of Ireland beach in August.

If you are making the stuffing especially for the pie, you may prefer to lose the fruit from the stuffing and just go porky. It's up to you.

serves 6

for the shortcrust pastry
170g/6oz plain flour
pinch of sea salt
85g/3oz chilled butter, cut
into cubes
1–2 tbsp cold water

for the filling
1 quantity sausage stuffing
(see page 9, or use the
alternative below)

Preheat the oven to 190°C/Gas 5. Sift the flour and salt into the food processor, add the butter cubes and pulse until the mixture resembles crumbs. Add 1 tbsp water through the feeder tube and process briefly until the dough forms a ball, adding more of the water as necessary. Wrap in cling film and put it into the fridge to rest for 30 minutes.

Roll out the pastry on a lightly floured surface to a large round and use to line a 23cm/9 inch tart tin. Line the pastry case with a piece of greaseproof paper and a layer of dried beans and bake 'blind' for 15 minutes. Remove the paper and beans, then prick the pastry with a fork and return to the oven for 5 minutes.

Pile the stuffing mixture quickly and gently into the pastry case, smoothing it down with a spatula. Bake for about 30 minutes until the top is browned and the filling is cooked; it should not have dried out.

Leave the pie to stand for 10–15 minutes before serving. It goes very well with home-made tomato sauce (see page 174) or just a dab of English mustard. If serving cold, cool completely on a wire rack.

Pork and apple stuffing

This is a great alternative for a sausage pie or to stuff a roast chicken, or you may decide to make double to give you enough for both. Peel, core and slice 2 tart eating apples, such as Cox's. Finely chop 1 onion, 1 garlic clove and 2 thumbs of ginger. Heat 2 tbsp olive oil and a knob of butter in a large frying pan and gently fry the onion, garlic and ginger with the apples and a handful of torn sage leaves until the onion has softened. Take off the heat, let cool a little, then tear in a crustless thick slice of bread. Add 450g/1lb sausage meat and a beaten egg, mix together well and season judiciously.

Poaching a chicken and saucing it up

You may decide to stretch your chicken in a different direction and poach it to begin with rather than roast it. It is a lovely mild and gentle thing to do with a good bird and you can still use any leftover meat for the lemon chicken risotto (on page 11) in the same way.

A simple cream sauce thickened with egg yolk and sharpened with lemon is wonderful with a poached bird and carries on the ivory coloured theme. You may serve the vegetables you have poached it with too and when the bird is stripped and done, plop the carcass back in the poaching liquor with a fresh set of vegetables to turn it to stock. Once strained, this doubly intense stock makes a lovely base for a soup, chicken or otherwise.

My absolute favourite way with a poached chicken is the dish opposite, chicken Savoyarde. Poaching also gives you the best textured meat for a chicken pie, in my case with a layer of buttery leeks and a béchamel made with half chicken stock, half milk and lots of celery, onion, parsley and mushrooms. That way less meat is needed, yet the pie is big on flavour.

Chicken stock

If you are using the carcass from a roasted chicken for your stock, then it is worth roasting the bones to intensify the flavour, keeping the fat and skin on the bird for added flavour. That is if you can be bothered. Sometimes I do, sometimes I don't. The bones from a poached chicken are not worth browning, as they aren't dry enough.

Don't worry if you don't have all the suggested vegetables for your stock, just use extra of the ones you do have. If you haven't used the chicken giblets for gravy, throw them in the pot too.

Place your stockpot over a lively heat, hurl in the bones and broken-up carcass and brown on all sides for a few minutes, or do this in the roasting tin in a hot oven instead if you'd rather, then transfer them to the pot.

Add a large onion, skin on for flavour and colour, halved and spiked with 2 cloves; a fat leek, cleaned, in half; a large carrot in chunks; 2 celery stalks with their leaves, broken into shorter lengths; a bouquet of parsley, thyme, rosemary and bay; and enough water to cover. Bring to the boil, skim off any scum from the surface and turn down to a low simmer, putting the lid on. Cook at a gentle burble for 2 hours.

Leave to cool in the pot, then strain the stock into a large bowl, cover and put into the fridge. When the fat has solidified, skim it off. Now your stock is ready to use.

Chicken Savoyarde

This is a dish for a special occasion and the quality of the ingredients is paramount. It is the first thing I cook when the autumn chill descends on us and we want a hearty dinner that boasts creamy richness, but is still one step short of the ballast one needs in winter. It has given more pleasure to more people than any other dish I can think of, and to me, the cook, too. Loyal followers who have come across it before, please spare a thought for new readers. It is my classic favourite. All you'll need to accompany it is steamed broccoli and some potato and celeriac purée. Something green is important, for colour on the plate.

Don't be put off by the amount of tarragon, a herb that is inclined to overwhelm with the taste of aniseed. Here, mellowed by the Gruyère, cream and white wine, it finds its own strength and subtlety to perfection, without stealing the show.

serves 6 (and some to spare)

to poach the chicken

1 organic or at least free-range chicken, about 2–2.25kg/4½–5½lb

2 onions, peeled and each stuck with a clove

2 large carrots, peeled and cut into chunks

3 celery stalks, cut into chunks

green tops of 2–3 leeks, well washed

a small bunch of herbs (thyme, rosemary, parsley and 2 bay leaves), tied together

6 peppercorns

for the sauce

55g/2oz butter

55g/2oz plain flour

400ml/14fl oz reserved poaching stock (from the chicken)

300ml/½ pint dry white wine, warmed

240ml/8fl oz double cream, warmed

100g/3½oz Gruyère, grated

1 tbsp Dijon mustard

55g/2oz tarragon leaves, chopped

sea salt and black pepper

for the topping

55g/2oz breadcrumbs

30g/1oz freshly grated Parmesan

To poach the chicken, put the bird into a heavy-bottomed pot in which it fits cosily and surround with the vegetables, herbs and peppercorns. Just cover with cold water. Bring to the boil, skim off any scum from the surface and turn the heat down to a low simmer. Cover and poach gently for about 1¼–1½ hours. The water must be at a bare shudder.

Either cool the bird in its poaching liquor or, if you are serving the dish immediately, remove it to a board and strain the stock into a bowl, discarding all the solids. Leave it to settle, then remove the surface fat.

Strip all the meat from the chicken if you are using it all for the dish; if not, enough for 6. Discard the skin and tear the meat with the grain into long, thinnish strips. Preheat the oven to 220°C/Gas 7.

To make the sauce, melt the butter in a pan, stir in the flour and let it bubble for a couple of minutes until it turns a light biscuit colour. Gradually add the hot poaching stock, a ladleful at a time, alternately with the wine and cream, whisking to keep the mixture smooth. When all of the liquid has been added and the sauce has been cooking for around 20 minutes so it has no residual floury taste, add the Gruyère, mustard, tarragon and some seasoning.

Continue to cook the sauce over a low heat for about 15–20 minutes. Taste and adjust the seasoning and mustard if you need to, then consider the balance of cheese, cream and wine, which should each have their place without being predominant.

Put the chicken into a gratin dish and pour over the sauce. Sprinkle with breadcrumbs and then with Parmesan. Bake for 20–25 minutes until the top is golden brown and bubbling with little eruptions of sauce bursting through. Wait 10 minutes before serving.

Mince

As always, it is all about quality, not quantity. Lesser mince – invariably watery and more fatty than anything you will buy from a good butcher – cannot be transformed into a great dish by sprucing it up with spices, vegetables or anything else for that matter. Far better to buy good butcher's mince and use it more sparingly. The organic longhorn beef I buy by the quarter-steer from a local farmer works out no more expensive than endless trips to the supermarket shelves for vastly inferior meat.

My ragù sauce has onion, carrot, celery, garlic and enough tomato – at least 2 tins to a half-kilo of meat – to flavour and colour the final sauce, after 3 hours simmering, with the richest and deepest of tones. That way, what might serve 2 or 3 people if you're majoring on meat, feeds 6. They won't complain for lack of meat when they've got the powerful alchemy of slow-cooked good ingredients to contend with on the plate, and all the flavours have married into an oily-rich intensely flavoured dish that bears no resemblance to, well, mince.

Even if you don't have a mincer, and I don't, you can do the next best thing with the remains of your leg or shoulder of lamb and chop it as small as small can be. I always buy shoulder, not just because it is more economical, but because I love the more intense, fattier flavour.

Obviously cooked minced meat is a different beast to deal with to the raw stuff, but only in terms of its cooking time and texture, which will never be quite so absorbent or malleable as starting from fresh. Just think of it as a different dish.

Shepherd's pie, cottage pie

This is the classic Monday night supper after a Sunday roast if you've cooked a joint of lamb or beef larger than you need, which I invariably do. Depending on how much meat you have left, adjust the amount of vegetables and potatoes accordingly. And keep back some dark gravy rich with meat juices so that you can intensify the flavour of the meat without stock.

In the autumn or winter, a cottage (beef) or shepherd's (lamb) pie made with half parsnip and half potato mash is a lovely variation – grate over some strong Cheddar too, if you like. And do try my alternative cottage pie (illustrated).

serves 4

675g/1½lb or thereabouts cooked beef or lamb, left over from a roast

3 tbsp olive oil

1 large onion, peeled and finely chopped

2 celery stalks, de-strung with a potato peeler and finely chopped

2 medium carrots, peeled and finely diced

3 garlic cloves, peeled and chopped

2 tbsp tomato purée

a few shakes of Worcestershire sauce

a few drops of Tabasco

2–3 anchovies, finely chopped (optional)

150ml/¼ pint or thereabouts gravy, left over from the roast

1 glass red wine (whatever is open)

1kg/2¼lb floury potatoes, such as King Edward's, or half potato, half parsnip or celeriac

55g/2oz butter or more, plus extra for dotting on top

150ml/¼ pint hot milk, or more

sea salt and black pepper

nutmeg for grating

2 tbsp coarsely grated strong Cheddar (optional)

Mince the meat or chop it very small by hand. Heat the olive oil in a large, heavy-bottomed frying pan and throw in the onion, celery, carrots and garlic. Stir over a medium heat until they begin to soften and turn translucent, about 7 minutes.

Add the meat and stir to brown evenly, over a livelier heat. After about 5 minutes, add the tomato purée, Worcestershire sauce and Tabasco to heat things up a little. Add the anchovies if using, mashing them in with a fork – they will bring out the flavour of the meat without making it taste at all fishy.

Stir the gravy into the meat mixture and then add the red wine. Simmer gently for about an hour to bring all the flavours together.

About 20 minutes before the end of the cooking time, preheat the oven to 200°C/Gas 6. Boil the potatoes and any roots separately in the usual way until tender. If using potatoes only, drain and mash with the butter and hot milk. If using parsnip or celeriac with the potatoes, you will not need milk, just mash them together with butter and a little of the root's cooking water. Season the mash, adding a little nutmeg too.

Put the meat into a baking dish, cover with the mash and scatter over the grated cheese if using. Dot the top with little flecks of butter. Bake for 30–40 minutes or until browned in patches and bubbling.

Serve with frozen peas and tomato ketchup. How could you do otherwise, this is proper Monday night food!

Alternative cottage pie

I made this discovery one evening when I was short of potatoes and lacking a few other ingredients. It was the best cottage pie ever.

Omit the carrots if you haven't any, but include the anchovies. Use 2 tbsp tamari sauce in place of the Worcestershire sauce for a lovely depth and complexity of flavour. If you haven't any wine open, add a splash of white port, Marsala or Madeira instead. Tip in a 400g/14oz tin of tomatoes and simmer everything together for 2½ hours, as you would for a ragù.

For the mash topping, use one-third celeriac to potato and stir through 2 sautéed, sliced leeks (the green part and the white).

Italian meat loaf

If you think this sounds too big for you or your family, remember, not only does it freeze well, but it is also portable picnic food and works brilliantly in a sandwich with some English mustard or mango chutney. Eke it out.

Inspect your fridge for this dish, as really it's the odds and ends of cheese, ham or bacon, tomatoes and eggs that you can change around, deciding on what stratum you are going to run like a seam through the meat. Green olives are great with pork or veal mince, a few capers tucked in are good with the parsley, so is a little anchovy with the egg, or Fontina as your melting cheese if you don't have a heel of Gruyère or Comté.

serves 8–10

450g/1lb beef or veal mince

450g/1lb pork mince

4 organic large eggs, beaten

2 large garlic cloves, peeled and finely chopped

1 large onion, peeled and very finely chopped

2 tbsp chopped flat-leaf parsley

1 tsp chopped thyme, or you can use tarragon or sage

sea salt and black pepper

3–4 plum tomatoes, skinned, deseeded and sliced

3 organic large eggs, boiled for 6 minutes, cooled, shelled and sliced

200g/7oz fried smoked bacon or pancetta, or prosciutto, ham or speck

18 or so large green olives, pitted and chopped (optional)

1 tbsp capers, rinsed, drained and chopped (optional)

6 anchovies, drained and finely chopped (optional)

30g/1oz each grated Parmesan and either Gruyère or Comté

Preheat the oven to 150°C/Gas 2. Oil a terrine or loaf tin, about 30 x 10cm/12 x 4 inches and 10cm/4 inches deep.

Put all the mince into a large mixing bowl with the beaten eggs, garlic, onion and herbs. Season generously and mix well with your fingers. Pack half the mixture into the prepared mould.

Layer the tomato slices over the mince mixture, then the sliced boiled eggs. Chop or finely slice the bacon or ham and arrange on top. Combine whatever optional store-cupboard items you are using and scatter over the meat, then sprinkle with the grated cheeses.

Pack the rest of the mince mixture down firmly on top and lay a sheet of greased greaseproof paper on the surface. Put the lid on, or cover tightly with foil if you are using an open loaf tin. Boil the kettle.

Stand the terrine or loaf tin in a roasting tin and pour in enough hot water to come halfway up the sides of the mould. Cook on the middle shelf of the oven for 1 hour. Uncover and bake for a further 15–30 minutes until browned on top and cooked right through. Insert a skewer into the centre of the loaf to check that it is cooked.

Serve hot, with tomato sauce and buttered boiled or jacket potatoes, or cool in the tin and serve cold.

If you have any leftover mince mixture, roll it into small walnut-sized balls, pushing a knob of mozzarella into the centre of each. Lightly roll in flour and fry, turning, until evenly coloured and cooked through, adding some tomato sauce (see page 174) for the last 5 minutes of the cooking time to heat through with the meatballs. Serve with pasta and pass around grated Parmesan.

Too much mash

You can never have too much mash. I defy you to. I can eat epic quantities of it when it is made with floury potatoes, rich Jersey milk and lovely French or Italian butter, stirred in with Maldon salt and a good scrunch of black pepper. My personal best was after running a marathon – the great white mountain on the plate disappeared in record time too. It felt like a kilo, but that day, for once, I knew I'd earned my excess.

For my mash, I put the hot potatoes through the coarse blade of a mouli straight back into the pan in which they were boiled, having melted the butter and heated the milk in the pan while the potatoes are in the mouli. I do it over a gentle heat and stir everything together with a wooden spoon.

Colcannon and champ, those simple, special Irish ways with spuds, really cannot be bettered. Spring onions softened in hot milk for champ, and cooked cabbage and leeks for colcannon (see page 57). For total indulgence, pour a stream of yellow melted butter into a crater on the summit of the mash for you to stir in with your fork.

There are so many simple, yet wondrous, things to do with mash second time around, it is worth making far, far too much so that there is no danger of eating it all at the first sitting, and every danger of having the base for tomorrow's breakfast, lunch or supper sitting there ready for you.

Think of a crisply fried potato cake, or potato and celeriac cake, of creamy crêpes Parmentier, the most delectable of potato pancakes, which will hold anything from black pudding to smoked eel, from crisp bacon to chicken livers. Or frazzle a little leftover cabbage in butter with grain mustard and you've a bubble and squeak to drape a few bacon rashers over or serve with a sausage.

If you are using leftover mash, don't keep it in the fridge over-night as something horrid happens to it, flavour-wise. Instead keep it covered in a cool larder or similar. Here are some of the things I love turning old, cold mashed potato into, such good things that nobody would even guess at their being yesterday's remains.

Potato bread

For this recipe you need only a mound of leftover mashed potato to make the most delectable breakfast treat: potato bread or potato farls. It is a real Irish comforter to smother with melting butter and scrunch a little pepper over. Or serve the warm triangles with a few slices of crisply fried black pudding or eggs, bacon rashers or a sausage, to make you remember how breakfast ought to be.

My Northern Irish neighbour Patricia rushed through the door one bitterly cold morning with a little foil package of warm, buttered farls for elevenses. I tucked into one and felt better immediately. This is her recipe.

serves 3 (or 2 greedies)

225g/8oz mashed potato
55g/2oz plain flour
pinch of sea salt
extra flour for dusting
butter and black pepper
to serve

Push the mashed potatoes through a potato ricer or sieve into a bowl and sift in the flour. Season with salt and mix thoroughly. Bring together with your hands to make a ball.

Dust your worktop with flour and roll out the dough to roughly a 20cm/8 inch circle. Cut out 6 triangular wedges, as you would a cake.

Put a cast-iron or other heavy-bottomed frying pan over a moderate heat for a few minutes to heat up. Dust lightly with flour and put the farls snugly in the pan. Cook for about 10 minutes until golden brown; they won't brown evenly. Turn over and repeat.

Remove to a wire rack and allow to cool slightly for a minute, then rub on butter until it melts and grind over some pepper. Eat straight away.

Eva's potato apple cake

The same neighbour, Patricia, of the previous potato bread says this cake would have been cooked in poor households all over Ireland during the early 1900s on a griddle over an open fire. It was very much a high days and holidays treat and Patricia's mother Eva made it frequently. Sadly, she has now passed away so it has become Eva's potato apple cake.

The idea that leftover mash was considered a luxury, along with a few Bramley apples and sugar, may be a thought somewhat alien to our times, but it is how I like to see food, be it the simplest, the poorest perceived ingredients. It reminds me of a trip I made to Puglia in Italy, region of 'la cucina povera' (the poor kitchen, peasant food), based almost entirely on vegetables and bitter weeds, and 'tostata' – the chaff left behind from harvesting, which is toasted and turned into pasta the colour of wild mushrooms. It is as exciting a cucina as any I have sampled and as full of simple, unusual, inexpensive treats as this apple and potato one is to the Irish.

serves 4

450g/1lb mashed potato
110g/4oz plain flour, plus extra to dust
pinch of sea salt

for the filling

2 large Bramley apples
55g/2oz unrefined vanilla caster sugar

Push the mashed potatoes through a potato ricer or sieve into a bowl and sift in the flour. Add the salt and mix thoroughly. Bring together with your hands to make a ball.

Divide the dough in half and roll out one half into a 20cm/8 inch circle, placing it on a lightly floured plate. On a floured surface, roll out the second ball to a round just a little larger than the first.

For the filling, peel, quarter, core and finely slice the apples into a bowl. Scatter over the sugar, turning the apple slices to coat them.

Pile the apple mixture on top of the dough round on the plate, leaving a border free around the edge. Using a pastry brush, dampen the edge with a little water. Put the second dough round on top and press the edges firmly together to seal.

Heat a shallow, heavy-bottomed or cast-iron pan over a moderate heat for a few minutes. Scatter a little flour over the surface. Carefully slide the potato cake into the pan and cook for 15–20 minutes until golden.

Slide the cake out of the pan and back onto the plate, then invert onto another lightly floured plate. Slide the cake back into the pan to cook the other side for 15–20 minutes.

Carefully transfer to a warmed serving plate and serve in wedges with thick cream – clotted if you can get it.

Parmesan potato cake
with mozzarella and prosciutto

I have adapted this beautiful dish from a recipe of the great Anna Del Conte. You may start with freshly made mash if you like, but it really is as good to use yesterday's. You just need to think ahead and add the butter, milk, nutmeg, Parmesan and eggs when you originally make the mash so that everything melts in properly.

It is a warming lunch or supper dish that works well served with some slow-cooked gratinéed tomatoes and a green salad. Ashamed of the idea of serving a souped-up potato cake for a supper party? You won't be with this dish, particularly if you use really good ingredients like a proper aged Parmigiano-Reggiano and San Daniele or a good prosciutto.

serves 4

850g/scant 2lb floury potatoes, peeled and cut into large chunks

100ml/3½fl oz hot full-cream milk

85g/3oz butter

sea salt and black pepper

a suspicion of freshly grated nutmeg

6 tbsp freshly grated Parmesan

3 organic large eggs, plus an extra yolk, beaten

a 400g/14oz mozzarella di bufala campana, sliced

85g/3oz prosciutto, about 6 slices

85g/3oz mortadella or salami (a salami with fennel seeds works well)

1 tbsp chopped flat-leaf parsley (optional)

for the base and top

4–5 tbsp stale breadcrumbs (brown or white)

20g/¾oz butter

Preheat the oven to 200°C/Gas 6. Boil the potatoes in the usual way until they are cooked through, then drain and mash well, adding the hot milk and butter. Season and add the nutmeg and Parmesan. Mix well, then add the beaten eggs and extra yolk and mix again. Set aside.

Butter a 20cm/8 inch springform cake tin and scatter over about a third of the breadcrumbs. Spoon over half the potato mixture. Cover with the sliced mozzarella, prosciutto, mortadella or salami, and parsley if using.

Spoon over the rest of the potato mixture, then sprinkle with the rest of the breadcrumbs and dot with butter.

Bake for about 30 minutes until the potato cake is browned and crisp on top and bubbling in the middle. Let it stand on a wire rack for 10 minutes before unhinging the side of the tin and removing it.

Cut the potato cake into thick wedges like a cake. Serve with a simple endive salad, dressed with a vinaigrette, and slow-cooked tomatoes on the side.

Chick peas

Always soak more than you need. Lovely leguminous things work as well on the side as they do mainstream, it's just a question of thinking them through. If you soak and cook a packet of dried chick peas, you can turn a third into creamy hummus and make soups, salads and stews with the rest, or even stuff peppers with chick peas and Indian-style spices.

If you love falafel (see page 33), you may wish to soak half of your chickpeas for rather longer as these tasty morsels are made from the raw peas, which require a full 24 hours soaking.

Here's what to do with the humble beady chick pea.

Hummus and chick peas to spare

I don't understand the false economy of supermarket hummus – I've simply never tasted one that didn't remind me of wallpaper paste. Soaking pulses is not, after all, hard work. Unless you've a crowd to feed, just use a third of the chick peas for the hummus and keep the rest in their gelled cooking liquor in the fridge for up to 3 days to use for other dishes.

to cook the chick peas

450g/1lb chick peas, soaked in cold water for at least 8 hours

1 onion, spiked with a clove

handful of leek tops, a celery stalk and a carrot (or any of these)

6 peppercorns

2 bay leaves

for the hummus

1–2 lemons

1–2 tbsp tahini paste (the toasted sesame paste is ideal)

2–3 garlic cloves, peeled and chopped

4–5 tbsp olive oil

sea salt and black pepper

1 tsp cumin seeds, toasted and crushed (optional)

splash of good extra-virgin olive oil

a small handful of coriander leaves, chopped (optional)

Drain the chick peas and tip into a heavy-bottomed pot. Add enough water to cover by about 2cm/¾ inch, but don't add salt at this stage. Add the flavouring vegetables, peppercorns and bay leaves. Bring to the boil, lower the heat and cover. Simmer until tender, 1½–2 hours depending on the age of the chick peas.

To make the hummus, put one-third of the chick peas into a blender with 2–3 tbsp of the cooking liquor. To begin with, add the juice of 1 lemon, 1 tbsp tahini, 2 garlic cloves, 3–4 tbsp olive oil, some seasoning, and the cumin if you are using it. Blitz to a purée.

Now taste critically. You will probably need the juice of at least another ½ lemon, some more salt, and possibly a little more tahini, though there should be a hint, not a hit, of this. Assess the garlic too; it shouldn't overwhelm but you should know it's there. You may need to let the purée down with a little more cooking liquor and a little more olive oil. It is down to your palate, how you like it best.

When you are happy with your hummus, scrape it into a small terrine or bowl and mark with the top of a knife to give you a ridged surface. Now swirl a little peppery green olive oil over the surface.

Either cover and keep in the fridge for a few days and use as needed or serve at once, with griddled pita bread or raw crunchy vegetables. A little freshly chopped coriander strewn over the top of the hummus before you serve it will alleviate the desert colour.

Chorizo and chick pea stew
with piquillo peppers

Oh the bliss of a quick supper where the initial cooking has been done and you just need to fry an onion and do a little simmering. The smoky, the piquant, the controlled heat and the earthiness of the individual components transform this dish into a hearty, tasty peasant Spanish stew. Eat it straight from the bowl, no extras needed and it's just as good the following day.

serves 6

400g/14oz chick peas, soaked in cold water for at least 8 hours

750ml/1¼ pints vegetable or chicken stock

300ml/½ pint passata

2 tbsp olive oil

2 medium onions, peeled and finely chopped

600g/1¼lb good-quality chunky chorizo sausage, cut into bite-sized chunks

3–4 garlic cloves, peeled and finely chopped

225g/8oz jar wood-roasted piquillo peppers (I use Navarrico), or use skinned, grilled fresh red peppers

1 tsp smoked paprika

sea salt and black pepper

a handful of flat-leaf parsley, chopped

Cook the chick peas in the stock and passata in advance until tender, about 1½–2 hours (or you can use ready-cooked chick peas, see note).

Heat the olive oil in a heavy-bottomed pan and gently fry the onions until softened. Throw in the chorizo and fry, turning the chunks as you go, for about 10 minutes. When the chorizo starts to release its characteristic red, oily fat, add the garlic, then the chick peas along with their liquor.

Cut the peppers into long, thin strips and add them to the pan with the smoked paprika. Simmer gently for another 10 minutes, then taste and season. Ladle into bowls and sprinkle over some parsley.

Use double the weight of ready-cooked or tinned chick peas; add the passata to the stew with them.

Chick pea and smoked paprika soup

This is something to make in a hurry with your leftover chick peas when you want a hearty, simple soup and don't have any time or any stock. Don't overdo the smoked paprika – it should exude a slightly smoky mystery to the soup, not the obvious taste of full-blown paprika.

serves 4

1 tbsp olive oil

1 red onion, peeled and finely chopped

3 garlic cloves, peeled and finely chopped

2 celery stalks, de-strung with a potato peeler and chopped small

2 tsp finely chopped rosemary needles

4 ladlefuls cooked chick peas

⅓–½ tsp smoked paprika

2 bay leaves

1 level tbsp tomato purée

400g/14oz tin cherry tomatoes

8–10 ladlefuls water, or use stock if you have it

sea salt and black pepper

a small handful of flat-leaf parsley, chopped

Heat the olive oil in a large, heavy-bottomed pan and add the onion, garlic, celery and rosemary. Fry for a few minutes until they begin to soften, then add the chick peas, smoked paprika, bay leaves, tomato purée and tinned tomatoes. Bring to a simmer, then add the water, season and bring back to the boil. Lower the heat and simmer for 10 minutes.

Discard the bay leaves. Blitz about half the mixture in a blender, then re-introduce it to the chunky soup in the pan. Taste and adjust the seasoning, stir in the parsley and reheat if you need to. Ladle into warm bowls and serve.

Falafel with tahini cream sauce

These little fried, spiced chick pea balls are great served with drinks or as a picnic snack. They are especially good dipped into the tahini cream sauce, but you can simply serve them with yoghurt flavoured with a crushed garlic clove, 1 tsp toasted, ground cumin and some seasoning if you prefer.

As the chick peas are used raw, you need to remember to put them to soak a full 24 hours ahead.

makes about 24

225g/8oz chick peas, soaked in cold water for 24 hours

1 large onion, peeled and finely chopped

3 garlic cloves, peeled and finely chopped

2 green chillies, deseeded and finely chopped

1 red chilli, deseeded and finely chopped

a handful of flat-leaf parsley, chopped

a handful of coriander leaves, chopped

2 tsp cumin seeds

2 tsp coriander seeds

sea salt and black pepper

600ml/1 pint groundnut or grapeseed oil, for shallow-frying

tahini cream sauce

2 garlic cloves, peeled

juice of 2½–3 lemons

150ml/¼ pint tahini paste

2 tbsp live goat's, sheep's or cow's milk yoghurt

about 2–3 tbsp cold water

1 tsp toasted cumin seeds, ground

a handful of flat-leaf parsley, chopped

Drain the chick peas and dry them on a clean tea-towel. Shoot them into the food processor with the onion, garlic, chillies and chopped herbs. Grind the cumin and coriander seeds in a mortar, then add to the blender with some seasoning. Blitz the mixture to a grainy-textured pulp; the chick peas will give it this texture. Tip into a bowl.

Take walnut-sized pieces of the mixture and form into little patties. You can either cook them immediately or keep them covered in the fridge until needed; they will be fine to cook the next day.

To make the tahini cream sauce, crush the garlic with a little salt. Put it into a bowl with 1 tbsp of the lemon juice and stir. Add the tahini and stir it in, followed by the rest of the lemon juice and the yoghurt. Add enough water, a spoonful at a time, to make a thick, smooth cream. Add the cumin and taste. The flavour needs to be tart and strong, so add a touch more garlic, lemon juice, salt or spice as needed.

When ready to eat, spoon the sauce into a bowl and sprinkle with the parsley. Heat the oil for shallow-frying in a heavy-bottomed pan. Drop a crumb of the falafel mix in to check that it is hot enough; it will resurface instantly and bubble away if it is. Fry the patties in small batches for about 4 minutes until deep golden brown, turning after a couple of minutes. Drain on a warm plate lined with kitchen paper.

Serve the hot, crisp falafel with the tahini cream sauce and warm pita bread if you like.

The tahini cream is a lovely sauce, by the way, to serve alongside a conventional roast shoulder or leg of lamb.

The Saturday bake

In this new age of packed-lunch fever, where we are growing more pumpkins than petunias for the first time ever, where we're reading seed packets not cornflake packets, sowing window-boxes, mulching tomatoes on roof terraces and saving our energy, there is no food that changes and nourishes our lives, our souls, more than baking.

Baking is the food of memory. Even if our mothers didn't stand us on the kitchen chair to sift flour, roll dough and prink jam tarts, it is a memory we all wish to have, imagine having. When we are children, when we are students, it is the form of cooking that most makes us grow in cooking confidence and it is the food that we like to eat. During childhood, our hearth and our hearts are in the kitchen; then, when we leave home, baking is the food that most reminds us of it. And it is the food we can afford as students. What price a stack of cookies, a sticky cake, a brownie, a warm, buttered tea loaf? We can bake with an almost empty pocket. We may not always feel like making the effort, but when we do we wonder why we don't more often.

When my friend Georgie talks about her childhood, she always goes back to the 'Saturday bake'. Money may have been scarce, but there was always a sense of plenty. Georgie's mother did all the baking for the week ahead with all four children. They made cornflake cakes and flapjacks, fairy cakes and butterfly cakes with wings, sticky ginger cake and shortbread dotted with cherries, currants or apple. At Sunday teatime there were sandwiches and cakes – always a fruit cake for Georgie's dad, which then went into the children's lunch-boxes every day – and usually a Victoria sponge spilling raspberry jam and cream. 'I never remember my mother buying a cake or a biscuit,' Georgie tells me.

When my three children were tiny my kitchen was really not very different. The smallest baby, Charissa, would be dangling from a kitchen ceiling hook in her baby bouncer or in the play-pen, Miranda and Harry up to no good somewhere in the garden, or once the scent of baking wafted past their nostrils, clambering to taste and decorate whatever I was making. Earliest toy? A wooden spoon.

Saturday afternoons were an immovable feast and still pretty much are: Geoffrey Smith's Jazz Record Requests blaring from Radio 3, the Kitchen Aid swirling, the Magimix whirring, the weekend's puddings and cakes, brownies and biscuits hitting the stove then the cooling rack. Wicked fingers will be trying to snitch a corner here, a crumb there, before the steam has fully escaped and a warm, damp cinnamon-tinged carrot cake is cool enough to cut.

Baking is the first cooking we do as children, with our children, and it really doesn't matter if they begin by only wanting to wipe the bowl and lick the spoon. A willing scoffer turns into a willing cook pretty quickly, and it is the only way to learn without feeling it's a lesson. Nobody is scared of making pastry if they don't know to be, nor do people fear a sponge not rising or a brownie not turning molten tender and gooey, if they take part in the process young and the family has a kitchen that's always ready and eager to bake in. So have your own bake-in and re-acquaint yourselves, if you need to, with one of the great joys of life: the Saturday bake.

Carrot cake
with lime and mascarpone topping

I have always loved a good, cinnamon-scented carrot cake but somehow found the normal butter icing too rich and too sweet for the cake. Carrots, after all, are sweet enough in their own right. However, this mascarpone topping – sharp and sherbetty with lemon and lime zest – contrasts perfectly with the texture and crunch of the carrots and walnuts. Take the path of least – if not no – resistance.

makes a 20cm/8 inch cake

180g/6oz plain flour

2 level tsp baking powder

1 tsp ground cinnamon, preferably freshly ground

½ tsp ground cloves

½ tsp freshly grated nutmeg

180g/6oz light muscovado sugar

150ml/¼ pint sunflower oil

2 organic large eggs

200g/7oz coarsely grated organic carrots

85g/3oz shelled walnuts, roughly chopped

for the topping

1 lime

200–225g/7–8oz carton mascarpone

100g/3½oz unsalted butter, softened

85–100g/3–3½oz unrefined icing sugar or light muscovado sugar

juice of ½ lemon, or to taste

Preheat the oven to 180°C/Gas 4. Grease and line one deep or two shallow 20cm/8 inch cake tins. Sift the flour and baking powder together into a large bowl and mix in the spices.

Using an electric mixer, whisk together the muscovado sugar, sunflower oil and eggs until smooth. With a large metal spoon, fold in the grated carrots and chopped walnuts, then fold in the flour and spices until evenly combined.

Spoon the mixture into the prepared cake tin(s), set on a baking tray and bake until a skewer inserted into the centre comes out clean; test after 25 minutes for sandwich cakes; 40 minutes for a deep cake. Leave to cool in the tin(s) on a wire rack.

For the topping, pare a few shreds of lime zest with a zester and set aside; grate the rest of the zest and squeeze the juice from one half. In a bowl, beat the mascarpone with the softened butter, sugar, grated lime zest, and the lime and lemon juices. Taste. I like a good sharp topping, so sometimes add more lime, sometimes more lemon juice.

Sandwich the cakes together with some of the mascarpone mixture if you have made two, or cut a deep cake into two layers. Spread the topping over the top of the cake and smooth it down the sides to cover completely, then ruffle the surface. Either refrigerate or serve immediately, topped with the reserved zest.
I like it a little cold, so that the icing has just set to a chill.

Add snowdrops in February!

Chocolate cake

Not another chocolate cake. Those are the words I am least likely to utter. The deadline for this manuscript is tonight. What do I do? I can't write a book without a new chocolate cake recipe in it. So I make one. Perhaps this will be the best chocolate cake I've ever made. Who knows?

I make it anyway, on a whim, I've had an idea for a lighter-than-normal cake with a hint of coffee and cassis, Marcona almonds, virtually no flour and lots of bitter chocolate. Charissa is stricken with mumps and can't swallow. That leaves me and Georgie. I'll call Patricia down the road and Pete the postman is bound to deliver! Oh yes, it's fabulous, everyone agrees, light as a soufflé and only minutes to get it to the oven.

makes a 20cm/8 inch cake

90g/3oz blanched Marcona almonds

150g/5½oz dark chocolate, about 72% cocoa solids (I use Green and Black's 'with added cocoa butter for easier melting')

1½ tbsp crème de cassis

2 tbsp strong espresso coffee

90g/3oz unsalted butter, cut into cubes

90g/3oz unrefined vanilla caster sugar

3 organic large eggs, separated

1 level tbsp plain flour (optional)

Preheat the oven to 160°C/Gas 3 and heat a baking sheet. Butter a 20cm/8 inch cake tin generously. Grind the almonds in a blender or food processor until just a little more coarse than finely ground.

Break up the chocolate and put into a heatproof bowl with the cassis and coffee. Melt over a pan of hot but not simmering water, making sure the bowl is not touching the water.

Add the butter, sugar and ground almonds and take the pan off the heat, keeping the bowl in place over the hot water. Stir the mixture until it is well amalgamated. Beat the egg yolks and stir them in until evenly combined.

In a clean bowl, stiffly whisk the egg whites. Scrape the chocolate mixture into a large bowl and stir in a spoonful of egg white. If adding the flour, sift it over the mixture and fold in. (Including the flour gives a slightly more coherent texture.) Fold in the rest of the whisked egg whites, a large spoonful at a time, as quickly and lightly as you can.

Spoon the mixture into the prepared tin and place on the preheated baking sheet on the middle shelf of the oven. Bake for about 50 minutes, but start testing the cake with a skewer after 40 minutes unless the middle is still obviously runny.

Leave to cool in the tin on a wire rack for 15 minutes, then push the base of the tin up from the sides and cool to warm.

Snaffle immediately, with or without crème fraîche or clotted cream. It will make your day. It is light and intense with a whiff of cassis and coffee. The edge has a slight crust, the middle is damp like a mousse.

Dried apricot upside-down cake

Dark, burnt sugar stickiness and sharp, unsulphured apricots make this cake as good for pudding as it is for tea. Substitute fresh apricots in season, otherwise this is a perfect store-cupboard recipe. You've probably got the ingredients already sitting there.

makes a 20cm/8 inch cake

for the topping

180g/6oz demerara sugar

125ml/4fl oz water

60g/2¼oz unsalted butter, cut into cubes

250g/9oz unsulphured dried apricots

for the cake

210g/7½oz plain flour

2 slightly rounded tsp baking powder

4 organic medium eggs

180g/6oz unrefined vanilla sugar

120g/4½oz unsalted butter, melted and cooled to tepid

Preheat the oven to 160°C/Gas 3. Grease a 20cm/8 inch springform cake tin.

To make the topping, dissolve the sugar in the water in a heavy-bottomed pan over a medium heat, stirring. Turn up the heat so that the sugar syrup bubbles and continue to cook until it is a dark mahogany colour and looks syrupy when you swirl it around the pan.

Remove the pan from the heat and carefully add the butter cubes; the mixture will fizzle and pop. Pour it directly onto the base of the prepared tin and quickly tilt and turn the tin to coat the base and a little way up the sides; it will set quickly. Arrange the apricots firmly in the burnt sugar base, in concentric circles.

For the cake, sift the flour and baking powder together. Whisk the eggs and sugar together using an electric mixer at full speed for about 10 minutes or until light, creamy, thick and trebled in volume. Add the sifted flour and fold in gently and lightly, using a spatula. Finally fold in the melted butter.

Spoon the cake mixture evenly over the apricots in the tin. Bake for 50 minutes or until a skewer inserted into the centre comes out clean.

Leave the cake in the tin on a wire rack to cool for 30 minutes or until the sponge has shrunk away from the sides of the tin enough for you to release it. Invert the cake onto a large plate. Eat warm with crème fraîche, or cold.

Almond cake with apricot jam

Home-ground Marcona almonds and a hint of bitter almond extract make this damp cake truly delectable. I have made it with a sharp hit of apricot jam, the sort that is good enough for the fruit to have kept shape and sharpness, and with Morello cherry jam, another of my favourites. Both work magic with almonds, it's up to you to choose. This is as good a pudding as it is a cake, so serve it with stewed fruit if you like – plums, rhubarb, apricots or figs.

makes a 20cm/8 inch cake

300g/10½oz blanched Marcona almonds

225g/8oz butter, softened

225g/8oz unrefined vanilla caster sugar

grated zest of 1 organic lemon

1 tsp natural almond extract

3 organic large eggs

120g/4½oz plain flour

1 heaped tsp baking powder

for the topping

3 heaped tbsp best apricot or Morello cherry jam (or raspberry or blackcurrant if you prefer)

2 tsp water

Preheat the oven to 160°C/Gas 3. Butter and flour a 20cm/8 inch springform cake tin. Grind the almonds in a blender or food processor until just a little more coarse than finely ground.

Cream the butter and sugar together thoroughly using an electric mixer until pale and fluffy. Fold in the ground almonds by hand, along with the lemon zest and almond extract. Now beat in the eggs, one at a time. Sift the flour and baking powder together over the mixture and fold in gently with a metal spoon.

Spoon the mixture into the prepared tin and bake on the middle shelf of the oven for about 55 minutes until a skewer inserted into the centre comes out clean, checking after 50 minutes. Leave in the tin on a wire rack to cool, then turn out onto a plate.

Melt the jam with the water in a small pan over a low heat and stir until just warm. Pour over the top of the cake and spread it around; it doesn't matter if it drips down the sides.

This cake keeps well as it is so damp with almonds. Serve it with or without crème fraîche.

Vanilla sugar

For a constant supply, save vanilla pods once you have used them – either whole to infuse custards etc, or after scraping out the seeds. Rinse and dry, then add to a large jar of sugar to impart fragrance and flavour. Keep adding pods to the jar as you use them – I have at least a dozen in mine!

Earl Grey fruit tea loaf

I first made this really fruity tea loaf with Fortnum and Mason's mixed dried fruits, which features dried strawberries, cranberries and cherries in addition to the more everyday golden sultanas. It may be beyond budget and location, but it certainly makes an everyday tea loaf special. I suggest you pick whatever combination of dried fruit appeals to you, but I will say that the mix of intensely sweet strawberry with sharp cherry and cranberry is one to aim for.

Consider blueberries, sour cherries, unsulphured apricots and Muscat raisins – just a little more exciting than currants, raisins and sultanas. And the leaf tea is as important, its bergamot or smokiness being absorbed by the fruit; choose Earl Grey or Lapsang leaves of the best you can muster. A miniature of whiskey glugged into the overnight mix can only add to the general pleasure.

This tea loaf keeps beautifully – wrapped in greaseproof and foil, or in a sealed tin for up to a week. It also freezes well, so you might like to double up and make two. Slice and butter, or toast for breakfast.

Remember to start the recipe a day ahead as the fruit needs to steep overnight in the tea.

makes a 900g/2lb tea loaf

400g/14oz mixed dried fruit, such as Muscat raisins, unsulphured apricots, strawberries, cranberries, cherries

120g/4½oz dark muscovado sugar

300ml/½ pint hot Earl Grey or Lapsang tea, freshly made using 2 heaped tsp loose-leaf tea leaves

225g/8oz self-raising flour

1 organic large egg, beaten

Put the dried fruit and sugar into a large bowl. Once the tea has brewed for 3 minutes, pour it over the fruit. Turn a few times before you go to bed, just to keep all the fruit lubricated. Leave overnight, until well plumped.

The next morning, preheat the oven to 180°C/Gas 4. Grease and line a 900g/2lb loaf tin. Sift the flour over the fruit in the bowl and add the beaten egg, then fold everything together.

Spoon the mixture into the prepared loaf tin and bake for 1 hour, then turn the oven down to 160°C/Gas 3 and bake for a further 25 minutes or until a skewer inserted into the centre comes out clean.

Cool in the tin on a wire rack, then turn out. Wrap in foil or keep in an airtight container.

Chocolate brownies

No chapter on baking could eschew the brownie. I will try any good brownie recipe sent my way. After all, we are all seekers of perfection in chocolate heaven and need to believe we are just that much away from it each time. That way we have to try again.

You need a crumb but not a raw-looking crumb on the skewer when you test for doneness, and a skewer pushed into the centre not the edge of the cake please, as the outsides are always crumbier and less gooky.

makes 12–16

200g/7oz dark chocolate, 64–74% cocoa solids

4 tbsp strong, freshly made coffee, or 2 espressos, cooled until tepid

110g/4oz unsalted butter, softened

225g/8oz unrefined caster sugar

2 organic large eggs, plus an extra yolk

140g/5oz plain flour

1 rounded tsp baking powder

a handful of blanched whole hazelnuts (optional)

Preheat the oven to 180°C/Gas 4. Line the bottom and sides of a small baking tin, 30 x 22cm/12 x 8½ inch or thereabouts, with buttered foil.

Break up the chocolate and melt in a double boiler or in a heatproof bowl over a pan of hot water on a low heat, making sure the bowl is not touching the water. Take off the heat and stir in the coffee.

Cream the softened butter and sugar together thoroughly, using an electric mixer, until light and fluffy. Beat in the eggs, one at a time, then add the egg yolk. With the mixer still running, add the chocolate and coffee mixture, amalgamate and then switch off the machine.

Sift the flour and baking powder over the mixture and fold in, using a large metal spoon. Scrape the mixture into the prepared tin and level it with a rubber spatula. Push the whole hazelnuts, if using, into the mixture at intervals, so they just stand proud. Bake for about 25 minutes, then test with a skewer, as described above.

When ready, place the tin on a wire rack and leave to cool. Cut into squares in the tin before removing.

You may like to serve the brownies with a blob of crème fraîche or clotted cream, or you may prefer vanilla ice cream.

Banana blondies

It's as though, baking-wise, the blonde never got a look-in. How often are you offered a blondie rather than a brownie, or a banana blondie? Scarcity value aside, blondies are irresistible, every bit as gorgeous as their raven-coloured counterparts and so good with home-made vanilla ice cream. Adult only they are not; you will charm the children out of the trees or away from the screens with promises of either.

These banana babes are adapted from a recipe of baking legend, Dan Lepard, so their pedigree is top notch.

makes 16

300g/10½oz unrefined vanilla caster sugar

2 tbsp water

75g/2½oz Brazil nuts, roughly chopped

100g/3½oz unsalted butter

200g/7oz good white chocolate (I use Valrhona or Green and Black's)

2 bananas, roughly 200–225g/7–8oz

1 organic large egg, beaten

1 vanilla pod, split, seeds scraped out

200g/7oz plain flour

¼ tsp baking powder

Preheat the oven to 190°C/Gas 5. Line the base and sides of a 20cm/8 inch square baking tin with foil.

Put 75g/2½oz of the caster sugar into a small pan with the water. Dissolve over a medium-low heat, then bring to the boil and bubble until the sugar turns deep mahogany. To test, take a little of the syrup with a teaspoon and drop it into a glass of cold water: it should set to a hard ball.

Remove the pan from the heat and stir in the Brazil nuts, then immediately spread the mixture onto an oiled baking tray. Leave to cool, then chop the toffee finely.

Melt the butter and white chocolate in a double boiler or heatproof bowl over a pan of hot water, making sure the bowl is not touching the water. Take off the heat.

Mash the bananas in another bowl and mix in the rest of the sugar, the egg and vanilla seeds. Add the melted chocolate mixture and stir until smooth. Sift the flour and baking powder over the mixture, then fold in, together with the chopped nutty toffee.

Scrape the mixture into the prepared tin and bake for about 35 minutes until golden on top, with a faintly wobbly set. Test with a skewer: it should come out with a crumb, not a raw bit of gloop attached. Place the tin on a wire rack and leave to cool. Don't slice until cold.

Serve the blondies with crème fraîche to sharpen them up, or vanilla ice cream for total indulgence.

Wholemeal date scones

These are slightly heavier than plain scones, but sweet and nutty at the same time and great spread warm with butter for a proper breakfast. My neighbour Patricia brought round a little basket of them wrapped in a gingham napkin the morning the Oscars were announced last March. I had been up since dawn watching the news of my brother Daniel's triumph. All it needed was some Champagne and 'There Will Be Blood' orange juice and coffee to accompany the fruity scones.

makes about 10

120g/4½oz plain flour

120g/4½oz wholemeal flour

60g/2¼oz unsalted butter, cubed and softened

1 tbsp baking powder

½ tsp sea salt

1 tbsp muscovado or other sugar

120g/4½oz pitted Medjool or other dates, roughly chopped

150ml/¼ pint full-cream milk

Preheat the oven to 220°C/Gas 7. Sift the flours into a large bowl and tip in any bran left in the sieve at the end. Add the butter cubes and rub together with your fingertips as quickly as possible until you have a breadcrumb consistency.

Stir in the baking powder, salt and sugar, then throw in the dates. Make a well in the centre and add the milk, mixing all together with a palette knife to a soft dough.

Working quickly, turn the dough out onto a floured surface and very gently roll it out to a 2.5cm/1 inch thickness. Stamp out rounds with a 5cm/2 inch cutter or the rim of an upturned small tumbler and place on a greased baking sheet. Bake for 10–12 minutes, or until well risen and golden. Cool on a wire rack.

These scones are best eaten warm with good salted or unsalted butter according to your taste and mood.

Dried cranberry and cinnamon friands

These delightful little frivolities are perfect with coffee or tea, or serve a pile of them with ice cream and a bowl of mixed berries. You may prefer to make friands with fresh raspberries, blackberries, blackcurrants or gooseberries, but here you have a sharp hit of dried fruit from something sitting waiting in your store-cupboard. I make mine in the trays I use for individual Yorkshire puds or muffins, which are a little deeper than bun tins, though they will do too.

makes 10–12

170g/6oz unsalted butter

285g/10oz unrefined icing sugar, plus extra to dust

85g/3oz plain flour

140g/5oz ground almonds, preferably freshly ground Marcona almonds

1 tbsp grated lemon zest (from about 2 organic lemons)

1 tsp ground cinnamon

2 organic large egg whites

100g/3½oz dried cranberries

Preheat the oven to 200°C/Gas 6. Grease two 6-hole muffin tins. Melt the butter gently in a pan and cook until it is golden, not brown. Remove from the heat.

Sift the icing sugar and flour into a large bowl. Add the ground almonds, lemon zest and cinnamon and mix together, then stir in the egg whites. Pour in the melted butter and stir to combine.

Spoon the mixture into the greased muffin moulds and scatter over the cranberries. Bake for about 15 minutes until light and springy to the touch, then leave to cool on a wire rack.

To serve, sift a little extra icing sugar over the friands. The unrefined tastes so much better and more toffee-ish than the bright white.

Bay, honey and lemon cake

There is something about fragrant, glossy-leaved fresh bay – a pure infusion of hope and aromatics. We often flavour meats with it, but tend to forget its talent and natural affinity with fruit. Bay is lovely macerated in a citrus syrup for a winter fruit salad (see page 146) and in this unusual cake, the lemon-syruped leaves wreathing the top like laurel with the thinly sliced lemons.

I like the taste and texture of wholemeal flour in this cake, and its consistency when damp with the lemony syrup, but the choice is yours. If you are feeling particularly indulgent, you can spread home-made lemon curd between the two sponges and arrive at an even richer heaven.

makes a deep 20cm/8 inch cake

240g/8½oz Marcona almonds

340g/12oz unsalted butter, softened

170g/6oz light muscovado sugar

170g/6oz unrefined vanilla caster sugar

4 organic large eggs

grated zest of 3 organic lemons (save the juice for the drizzle)

340g/12oz wholemeal or plain flour, or half and half

2 tsp baking powder

pinch of sea salt

2 heaped tbsp live yoghurt, cow's, sheep's or goat's

for the drizzle

2 heaped tbsp strong-tasting runny honey, such as chestnut or acacia

1 organic lemon, finely sliced, plus the juice of 3 lemons (see above)

8–10 fresh bay leaves

60g/2oz demerara or unrefined granulated sugar

2 tbsp water

for the filling (optional)

about 5 tbsp home-made lemon curd

Preheat the oven to 180°C/Gas 4. Butter two 20cm/8 inch cake tins with removable bases and line the bases with greaseproof paper. Grind the almonds in a blender or food processor until just a little more fine than coarsely ground, to retain some texture.

Cream the softened butter and sugars together using an electric mixer until light and fluffy. Beat in the eggs, one at a time, then incorporate the lemon zest.

Sift the flour(s), baking powder and salt over the mixture, tipping in any bran left in the sieve, and add the ground almonds. Fold in with a metal spoon until evenly combined. Stir in the yoghurt, 1 tbsp at a time, to give a soft dropping consistency.

Divide the mixture between the prepared cake tins. Bake on the middle shelf of the oven for about 40–50 minutes until a skewer inserted into the centre comes out clean.

While the cake is baking, prepare the drizzle. Put the honey, lemon juice, bay leaves, sugar and water into a heavy-bottomed pan and stir over a low heat until the sugar has dissolved. Bring to the boil and bubble hard for 10 minutes or until you have a sticky syrup when you swirl it around the pan. Now add the finely sliced lemon, without pips. Bubble for 2–3 minutes, then remove from the heat, cover with a lid and leave to cool.

When the cakes are cooked, place the tins on wire racks and leave to cool for about 10 minutes. Now set a large tray or plate under the rack to catch any syrup that escapes. Spike holes all over the tops of the cakes with a skewer almost to the bottom and pour the syrup over slowly and carefully.

Either sandwich the cakes together with lemon curd or simply put one on top of the other. Deck the top with the slices of lemon and bay leaves from the syrup.

Lemon curd

Put 85g/3oz cubed unsalted butter, 225g/8oz unrefined granulated sugar and the grated zest and juice of 2 large organic lemons into a heavy-based pan and stir over a low heat until the sugar is dissolved. Stir in 3 beaten large eggs. Keep stirring, taking care not to overheat, until the mixture thickens, about 5–10 minutes. Pot instantly.

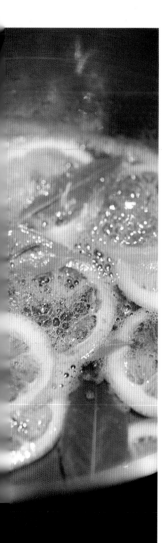

Butter biscuits

These are a little on the slender side to be shortbread, I feel, so I call them butter biscuits. They only take 5 minutes to make and are so much better than the commercial alternative. You can flavour the dough with a little grated orange zest and a few drops of orange oil, or chocolate chips if you prefer. Or, for the best summer version, finely chop 9–12 heads of lavender flowers and add them to the mixture. These lavender biscuits are especially good served with a fool or ice cream. In early spring, you can use rosemary flowers in the same way for an unusual variation. Stamp the dough into circles, half-moons or hearts, as the mood takes you.

makes 25–30

240g/8½oz unsalted butter, cut into cubes

150g/5½oz unrefined caster sugar

360g/13oz plain flour

flavouring (optional, see above)

demerara sugar or a little unrefined icing sugar, to sprinkle

Preheat the oven to 160°C/Gas 3. Blitz the butter, sugar and flour briefly in a food processor until the mixture forms a dough that just coheres into a ball. Add any flavouring ingredient (as suggested above) at this point and briefly work into the dough by hand.

Flatten the ball with your hand on a lightly floured worktop, then roll out to about a 5mm/¼ inch thickness. Use cutters to stamp out the shapes you want.

Lift the shapes onto a greased baking sheet with a palette knife, leaving a decorous gap in between. If you are using lavender or rosemary, press a short stem and its flowerhead gently into each one at this stage. If using demerara sugar, sprinkle evenly on top.

Bake for 10 minutes before checking. They may need up to 5 minutes longer, but should be faintly coloured around the edges.

Leave the biscuits on the baking sheet for 5 minutes to firm up, then slide a palette knife underneath and lift them onto a wire rack to cool. Sprinkle lightly with icing sugar unless you have sugared them before baking.

Pot luck: single pot

There is a whole genre of food that rejoices in coming together under a single roof. The 'one pot dinner' is its name. Yes, you may wish to cook rice or potatoes on the side or perhaps an extra vegetable, but the whole point of a stew or tagine, a pasta bake or pilau, a pot-roast, daube or braise is that you really have very little else to think about, timing is not too much of the essence, it cannot spoil easily and it is happy to fly solo. Lift the lid on it and you need look no further. It's the 'Aaaaah Bisto!' moment, metaphorically speaking, that is.

So the received wisdom of the day is that beef is bad, beef is red meat, beef is expensive. We only eat beef on Sundays. As far as I'm concerned, the prohibition gives me something valid to beef about. We know processed meats are bad for us, that sausages and bacon, salami and cured hams should be eaten in moderation. We know we shouldn't eat too much red meat. Producing it robs the earth of precious rainforest and water, and, as importantly, of more growing space for the humbler grains: rice, wheat, millet, corn; of the vegetables, cereals and fruits that need scant acreage and water supply in comparison in order to feed a far greater population for far less money.

We have the answer, yet we ignore the question, the problem. How foolish we will look, when people look back upon what we know now, and analyse why we were so resistant to do what was necessary for our survival, our health and the continuance of the planet.

Proselytising is going to get me nowhere, I know, but offering recipes that use the cuts of meat based on working muscle, skin and

dinners

bone – the true harbingers of flavour and texture – where the vegetables and grain are not mere counterpoint, they are the point, is what this chapter is all about.

Hock, belly, shank, marrow bone, oxtail, skirt, trotter, brisket and cheek... What have we done to our cuisine by limiting it to 'fast', no longer embracing slow? We have discarded some of the things we have cooked best of all throughout our culinary evolution, and now we are going to bring them back. Fiscal force majeure will see these classic cuts back on our plates, in our homes and in our cookery books, a reminder to people that chicken breasts are not the only meat.

The do's and don'ts of our edible etiquette seem to change daily and involve more rules than we are ever likely to enjoy hot dinners. So, I stick to the simple rules of the table:

Pleasure comes first, but not at any cost to the environment, the animal, the farmer or the pocket.

If you eat fewer processed foods you will automatically be eating better and for less, astonishing though that may seem.

Eat less and better and do less to your raw ingredients to make them taste better, taste more of themselves. The fewer and better the ingredients, the more vibrant and clear the flavours.

Entertain your friends royally but be proud to do it with the humblest of ingredients.

Invite them to a 'one pot dinner'. You really can't go wrong.

Beef stew with mustard and thyme dumplings

Chuck or braising steak, stewed long and slow in a bottle of red, with some lovely fluffy golf balls of green-flecked dumplings steamed on top – the very British answer to dim sum. You may prefer parsley and horseradish in your dumplings, but surprise heat is a must, so mustard or horseradish for bite and warmth.

serves 6

1.5kg/3¾lb braising or chuck steak

about 2 tbsp seasoned flour

2 tbsp olive oil

2 large onions, peeled and chopped

6 garlic cloves, peeled and left whole

sea salt and black pepper

4 celery stalks, de-strung with a potato peeler and sliced

4 large carrots, peeled and cut into chunks

2 large leeks, cleaned, whites cut into short lengths, green tops saved

1 small swede, peeled and cut into cubes

1 small celeriac, peeled and cut into cubes just before using (optional)

1 bottle robust red wine

400g/14oz tin whole tomatoes

a bouquet garni of parsley, thyme, rosemary, bay and 2 strips of orange peel, tied together

for the dumplings

110g/4oz self-raising flour

55g/2oz beef or vegetable suet

1 tbsp thyme leaves, chopped, or 2 tbsp chopped parsley

1 tbsp grain mustard or 1 tsp Colman's English mustard powder, or 2 tsp freshly grated horseradish

to serve

colcannon

Preheat the oven to 150°C/Gas 2. Cut the beef into large cubes. Tip the flour into a Ziplock bag, add the meat, lock and shake to coat. Take out the meat, shaking off excess flour. Heat about 1 tbsp olive oil in a large, heavy-bottomed pan and brown the meat in batches all over, removing it to a plate when browned and adding extra oil as needed.

Add the onions and garlic to the pan and sprinkle with a little salt. After a few minutes, as they begin to soften, add the celery, carrots, leeks, swede and celeriac, if using. Sauté for a few minutes and then return the meat to the pan. Meanwhile, heat the red wine.

Add the tinned tomatoes to the pan and chop them down into the meat and veg. When the liquid is bubbling away merrily, add the wine to just cover. Once the pot has come up to the bubble again, tuck the bouquet garni down into the depths, add a circle of greaseproof paper (a cartouche) to just cover the stew and put the lid on. Transfer to the oven and cook for 2 hours or until the vegetables are tender but not reduced to mush.

Meanwhile, make the dumplings. Sift the flour into a large bowl and throw in the suet. Add the herbs, mustard or horseradish and seasoning, and mix well together. Slowly add cold water, 1 tbsp at a time, and mix with your hands or a spoon until the dough coheres but is not too wet and sticky. If it becomes too damp, scatter over a little more flour and roll the ball of dough gently. Flour your hands and pull small, walnut-sized pieces of dough from the ball, rolling them between your palms into balls.

About 20 minutes before the stew will be ready, uncover and sit the dumplings on top. Put the lid back on and return to the oven. After 20 minutes, check that the dumplings have swollen and are cooked through. A couple of dumplings per serving is enough for all but the hardiest and heartiest of eaters. Don't forget the colcannon.

Colcannon

Slice a small Savoy cabbage into slim ribbons, add to a pan of fast-boiling water and cook for 5 minutes, then drain and refresh under cold water. Peel 6 medium potatoes, cut into chunks and boil (as for mash). Clean and finely chop the leek tops (saved from the stew), discarding any tough outer layer, and fry gently in butter until soft. Drain the potatoes and mash well, incorporating about 150ml/¼ pint hot full-cream milk and 90g/3oz butter. Reheat gently, stir in the cabbage and buttery leeks, adjust the seasoning and serve.

Brisket with pickled walnuts
and celeriac

This really is a complex flavoured dish, robust with meat, nuts and autumnal or winter veg. Celeriac works brilliantly, but in its absence add more celery and carrots, even some turnips if you like a bitter twist. Please improvise if you don't have any stock to hand and add a little more wine and some water instead.

Try to buy walnuts that have been pickled in proper wine vinegar, maybe with a little port or red wine too, or pickle them yourself in the shell if you are lucky enough to have a walnut tree in your garden. My tree is still a baby and not producing nuts yet; when it does, I will be on permanent squirrel alert.

serves 6–8 (depending on the amount of veg)

1.5kg/3¼lb piece of rolled, tied brisket of beef

a little flour

sea salt and black pepper

1 tbsp beef dripping, goose fat or olive oil

1 celeriac

3 onions, peeled and roughly chopped

6 medium carrots, peeled and cut into chunks

3 celery stalks, de-strung with a potato peeler and sliced

6 garlic cloves, peeled

550ml/18fl oz red wine and beef stock, about half of each

8 pickled walnuts, halved, plus 3 tbsp liquor from the jar

3 bay leaves

a sprig of rosemary

Preheat the oven to 150°C/Gas 2. Sprinkle the fat side of the brisket with a little flour and season with salt and pepper.

Heat a large, heavy-bottomed cooking pot into which the brisket will fit snugly, and then add the dripping, goose fat or olive oil. (If you have dripping left over from a roast, add the jellied dark juices below the fat too, for flavour.) When it is fizzing, put the brisket into the pot, fat side down, and allow it to brown for 3–4 minutes before rolling it over and browning the meat all over. Remove the meat to a large plate.

Peel the celeriac and cut into small chunks. Swiftly throw into the pot with the onions, carrots, celery and garlic and brown briefly on all sides, adding some salt and a good scrunch of pepper. (You need to prepare the celeriac just before cooking otherwise it will discolour.)

Meanwhile, heat the red wine and stock together in a small pan.

Skim off the excess fat from the surface, then put the meat back into the pot with the vegetables and pour in the hot red wine and stock. Add the pickled walnuts with their liquor and the herbs and bring slowly to simmering point.

Cut out a circle of greaseproof paper (a cartouche) and lay over the surface, then cover with the lid. Put the pot in the oven and cook for 2 hours before peeking and testing the vegetables and meat. It may take another 30 minutes for the meat to feel tender and the vegetables to be cooked through.

This dish can be made with braising steak cut into large pieces, about 6cm/2½ inches square and 2cm/¾ inch thick. Brown in the same way and then cook as above at a lower temperature, 140°C/Gas 1, for 4 hours.

Oxtail stewed with grapes

This is one of those dishes that is somehow jocund, beneficent and fruitful, and I simply have to make it at least once a winter. It is a heart-and-soul dish with the lovely autumn feel of the vineyard, where it is served in France at the end of the grape harvest. I have never known anyone, however tail-shy, not assault it with gusto, and love the coarse-textured grapey sauce with its sweetness and depth of flavour. This recipe is adapted from one of Elizabeth David's.

It is worth making it with at least two oxtails, or three, as it will both freeze and keep well in the fridge for a few days, and is great reheated.

Please start the day before if you have time so that the dish can cool and chill and you can then scrape the fat off and mouli the sauce.

serves 6–8

2 oxtails, chopped by your butcher

120g/4½oz piece unsmoked streaky bacon, snipped into small strips

2 large onions, peeled and chopped

4 large carrots, peeled and cut into small dice

2 celery stalks, de-strung with a potato peeler and chopped

6 garlic cloves, peeled

a bouquet garni of bay, parsley, rosemary, thyme and a strip of orange peel, tied together

sea salt and black pepper

2 whole allspice

about 600ml/1 pint red wine

1kg/2¼lb seedless green grapes

Preheat the oven to 140°C/Gas 1. Have the oxtail cut into pieces and ready to cook. Throw the bacon strips into a large, heavy-bottomed casserole and scatter the chopped vegetables and whole garlic cloves on top. Get the cooking process started over a low heat so that the fat starts to run from the bacon. Once it's all fizzling merrily, put the pieces of oxtail on top of the vegetables and bury the bouquet in their midst. Season and add the allspice, then pour over enough wine to just cover. Bring to a simmer before throwing in the grapes.

Cut out a circle of greaseproof paper (a cartouche) and lay it over the surface as the liquor comes back up to simmering point. Cover with the lid and cook in the oven until tender, about 3–4 hours, though longer won't harm. You can serve the dish straight away but it is best left to cool, then placed in the fridge overnight.

The following day, spoon off the solidified white fat from the surface and remove the meat to a plate. The liquor will have jellied delectably in the fridge. Discard the bouquet garni, then push the sauce through the coarse plate of a mouli. If you do not have a mouli, I suggest a quick blitz in a food processor, though it won't give you the uniformly coarse sauce that really gives this dish character. Check the seasoning and return the meat to the casserole with the sauce. Reheat slowly and simmer for a few minutes.

Serve in warm soup plates – the moat of sauce is what makes it – just some mashed potato on the side, you don't need another vegetable.

Braised belly pork with quince

Pork and apricots, pork and apple, pork and prunes... We know and love the sharp, soft fruits that add taste and acidity to the rich sweetness of pork, but what, I thought, about pork and quince? My tree hasn't yielded a solitary Aphrodite's apple yet, but the farmers' market has them in the autumn and then later in the winter they arrive from North Africa with the pomegranates, and how glad we are just to scent a room with one on a mantlepiece or poach them in syrup.

This dish worked miraculously, the belly and the fruit infusing and informing one another with a special magic. And the quince was turned to tenderness just when the meat fell from its little rib bones.

serves 4

1.2kg/2¾lb piece belly pork or thereabouts, ideally organic Middle White, scored

1–2 tbsp olive oil

sea salt and black pepper

2 quinces

juice of 1 lemon

600ml pear perry or good, dry cider

1 heaped tbsp blackstrap molasses

3 bay leaves

1 star anise

6 juniper berries, bruised

2 cloves

1 tbsp dark molasses sugar

1 tbsp acacia or other runny honey

Preheat the oven to 140°C/Gas 1. Lay the pork belly, rind up, on a board. Rub some olive oil into the rind with your fingers, then do likewise with salt and pepper. Leave the pork to stand in a cool place for 30 minutes to 1 hour.

Heat a little olive oil in a heavy-bottomed pan and add the pork, skin side down. The rind should seize and brown a little. Slide a knifepoint under the skin into the fat at intervals to encourage it to run a little.

Quarter the quinces, leaving their skins on, and core them. They will be very hard, so go carefully with the knife. Instantly dunk them all over in the lemon juice so that they don't discolour.

Take the pan off the heat and tuck the quinces snugly around the pork. Heat the pear perry or cider and pour it around the quinces and meat. Drip the blackstrap molasses over the belly, throw in the bay leaves, star anise, juniper berries and cloves, and sprinkle over the sugar and honey. Bring back to a simmer. Cover with a circle of greaseproof paper (a cartouche), cut to fit, and the lid. Cook in the oven for 2 hours.

Spike a quince quarter to see that it is tender, and if not return to the oven and test again after a further 20 minutes.

Serve straight from the pot. I like to serve mine with borlotti beans – soaked and cooked in half red wine and half water – with added cubes of celeriac fried in olive oil and rosemary. Potatoes or brown rice would also be good.

Sausage and mustard casserole
with cabbage and chestnuts

One of those lovely dishes where you simply cannot imagine the alchemy of the final result from the bog-standard ingredients you know so well.

I originally fell in love with Jane Grigson's 'cabbage in the Troo style' years ago for its utterly unpretentious marriage of pork and cabbage whose juices flooded, the one into t'other, and, with the aid of a little butter and much slow cooking, resulted in a cake of pink and green layers of succulent beauty.

I have added grain mustard from Gascony to mine and a wintry, mealy, rubble of chestnuts to the cabbage, but you can leave them out if you like. This is a dish of substance and will just need a jacket potato besides.

serves 4

6 good pork sausages

1 Savoy or other green cabbage

sea salt and black pepper

2 heaped tsp grain mustard

12–15 whole, peeled cooked chestnuts, from a 200g/7oz jar organic Sierra Rica chestnuts, or home-roasted or vacuum-packed, broken in half

knob of butter, about 25g/1oz

Preheat the oven to 140°C/Gas 1. Skin the sausages. Put a large pan of water on to boil. Finely slice the cabbage, wash and drain. When the water is boiling, throw the cabbage in, press it under the water and bring back to the boil. Boil for 3 minutes, then drain immediately in a colander and pour cold water over to refresh it and arrest the cooking process. Press out as much water as you can.

Grease a small casserole with butter and add a third of the cabbage. Season lightly (the sausages should be well seasoned). Press three of the sausages flat between your hands and place on top of the cabbage to create a complete layer. Spread the grain mustard over the sausage. Add a further third of the cabbage along with the chestnuts. Flatten the rest of the sausages to create another layer, then top with a final layer of cabbage.

Dot with butter and cover the surface with a butter paper or sheet of greaseproof and then the lid. Bake for 2–2½ hours, but longer won't hurt if you are playing for time.

Serve with jacket potatoes.

Orange-scented lamb
with chick peas, rice and yoghurt

I have long been an admirer of Afghani cuisine, albeit through a single tome, the delightful Noshe Djan of Helen Saberi. The ingredients are accessible and inexpensive, the cuisine not harshly nor pungently spiced, the gentle scent of orange peel and turmeric wafting through this dish with the dill as it comes to fruition.

It is a great stride away from the Mediterranean and Middle Eastern cuisines that we have absorbed and taken to our hearts over the last 50 years, which is, I feel sure, what drew me to it originally. It isn't like anything else I know. It is a cuisine of strength, simplicity, complexity of flavour and depth, marrying meat with rice, yoghurt and pulses – chick peas, mung bean, split peas – and with dried fruits – dates, apricots, prunes.

This is a late autumn and winter dish, everything cooked in a single pot and only a salad needed besides.

serves 6

750g/1¾lb or thereabouts lamb shoulder on the bone, cut into 3 large hunks

3 medium onions, peeled and finely sliced

1 tsp ground turmeric

1 large orange, sharp rather than sweet (I use Seville in season, or Tarocco from Sicily)

sea salt and black pepper

450g/1lb short-grain rice, washed and drained

500g/1lb 2oz carton live yoghurt, strained in a muslin-lined sieve

4 garlic cloves, peeled and smashed with the flat of a knife blade

1 tbsp olive oil

1 tbsp chopped fresh, or 2 tsp dried dill

400g/14oz cooked chick peas, drained (tinned if you must)

Preheat the oven to 140°C/Gas 1. Put the chunks of meat into a large, heavy-bottomed cooking pot with the sliced onions. Add enough water to cover. Sprinkle over the turmeric and bring to a simmer. Cover with a circle of greaseproof paper, cut to fit (a cartouche), and the lid. Cook in the oven for 3 hours or until the meat is tender and falls easily from the bones. Alternatively, cook gently on the hob over a very low heat, checking after a couple of hours.

While the meat is cooking, pare the zest from the orange. Cut it into matchstick strips and leave to soak in warm water.

When the meat is tender, remove it from the pot and tear into long thin shreds by hand, discarding the bones. Return the meat to the pot, season and add the rice. The liquid should cover the rice by about 2cm/¾ inch, so add more water if needed. Bring to the boil, then reduce the heat to a simmer and cook, with the lid off, stirring from time to time until the rice is al dente and the liquid is absorbed. You may need to add a little extra water as the rice is cooking.

Add the strained yoghurt, stirring it in thoroughly.

In a small pan, fry the garlic in the olive oil until pale golden, then add to the meat and rice. Drain the orange peel and add it too, along with the dill and chick peas. Mix all together and check the seasoning. Cover with the lid and leave on a very low heat for 30 minutes to allow the flavours to marry.

Lamb and kidney pudding
with a rosemary crust

I'm particularly pleased with this new dish. An old-fashioned suet crust is quick, easy and satisfying to make, yet so often overlooked on the basis that it is too heavy. Well, this turned out crisp and not too heavy, golden brown with flecks of rosemary, and the filling sealed inside imparted every last burst of intense flavour. The wine-dark gravy gave a whiff of kidney and garlic, a hint of redcurrant. I ate three helpings.

As for the cooking, it couldn't be easier. Shunt the pud in the oven in its bain-marie and forget about it for 2–2½ hours. If you have time, start the dish early so you can cool the filling before sploshing it into the crust.

serves 4–6

450g/1lb shoulder of lamb, trimmed of fat

3 lamb's kidneys, skin removed, halved and cored

1 tbsp seasoned flour

1½ tbsp finely chopped rosemary needles

2 tbsp olive oil

1 onion, peeled and finely chopped

3 garlic cloves, peeled and sliced

1½ tbsp redcurrant jelly

about 300ml/½ pint robust red wine

sea salt and black pepper

for the suet crust

285g/10oz self-raising flour

110g/4oz beef suet

1 tsp baking powder

1 level tbsp finely chopped rosemary needles

cold water to mix

Cut the lamb and kidneys into small cubes. Tip the seasoned flour and 1 tbsp chopped rosemary into a Ziplock bag. Add the lamb and kidney pieces, lock and shake to flour, then take out, shaking off excess flour.

Heat 1 tbsp olive oil in a wide, heavy-bottomed pan and throw in the rest of the chopped rosemary needles. When they fizz, after about 30 seconds, add the onion and garlic and sauté until the onion begins to soften and turn translucent. Remove to a plate with a slotted spoon.

Add the rest of the oil to the pan and fry the lamb and kidneys until browned all over. Add the redcurrant jelly and melt, then pour in half the wine. Let it bubble and reduce before adding the rest. Cook for 3–4 minutes, then season. If the juice looks too thick add a little more wine. Remove from the heat and allow to cool completely, if you have time.

Make the crust just before using. Preheat the oven to 180°C/Gas 4. Mix the dry ingredients together in a large bowl. Season and stir in 2–3 tbsp cold water to begin with, then 1 tbsp at a time, until the dough forms a ball. Flatten on a floured surface, then roll out to a large circle that will line a 1.2 litre/2 pint pudding basin. Cut out a quarter for the lid.

Ease the three-quarter circle into the greased pudding basin, leaving some overhang, and press the join together. Roll out the quarter piece to a round for the lid. Spoon the filling into the basin and top with the lid, pressing the edges together to seal and trimming as necessary. Cover the basin with a pleated sheet of greaseproof paper and foil. Tie string tightly around the rim, making a string handle at the same time.

Put the basin into a large casserole and pour in enough boiling water to come halfway up the side. Put the lid on and steam in the oven (or on the hob) for 2–2½ hours; it is not fussy time-wise.

Lift the pudding out and remove the foil and greaseproof paper. Leave for a few minutes to settle. Run a palette knife round the outside of the crust and then invert the pudding onto a hot serving dish – deep enough to contain the gravy. Serve with mash and cabbage or sprouts.

Chicken or rabbit cobbler
with sweet peppers and tomatoes

Chicken and rabbit can both handle strong accompanying flavours, so celery, red onion, garlic, tomatoes and roasted peppers are all in the picture, as are paprika and fruity olive oil. Garlicky sausage is included too, but you can leave it out if you prefer.

A crisp and fluffy cobbler of light biscuity scones, scented with thyme and Parmesan, adds substance and is a good instead-of if you feel like a spud-less supper. Note that cobblers need to be served up hot so that the cobbles don't lose their crisp and become sodden.

serves 6

4 red peppers, or use roasted piquillo pimentos from a jar (Navarrico wood-roasted are ideal)

3–4 tbsp olive oil

1 large chicken, jointed, legs and thighs separate, each breast in two, or if using rabbit, see note

1 large red onion, peeled and finely chopped

3–4 garlic cloves, peeled and sliced

3 celery stalks, de-strung with a potato peeler and chopped

a bouquet garni of 3 or 4 sprigs of thyme, 2 bay leaves and 2 strips of orange peel, tied together

450g/1lb coarse, garlicky sausage, or good butcher's sausages, cut into chunky bits (optional)

400g/14oz tin cherry tomatoes

½–1 tsp paprika

sea salt and black pepper

for the cobbler

225g/8oz plain flour

2 rounded tsp baking powder

100g/3½oz chilled unsalted butter, diced

4 tbsp freshly grated Parmesan or strong Cheddar, plus extra to sprinkle

6 sprigs of thyme, leaves stripped and chopped

170ml/6fl oz single cream or full-cream milk

Preheat the oven to 180°C/Gas 4. Char the red peppers all over under a hot grill, or by holding with a pair of tongs over a gas burner, then place in a bowl, cover with cling film and leave for 5 minutes or so (the steam will loosen the skins). Peel the peppers while still warm, remove the core and seeds and cut into strips.

Heat half the olive oil in a heavy-bottomed ovenproof pan and brown the chicken or rabbit pieces on all sides over a medium heat. Remove them to a plate.

Add the rest of the olive oil to the pan and sauté the onion, garlic and celery until just beginning to soften, then add the bouquet garni. Throw in the sausage chunks, if using, and brown on all sides briefly.

Return the chicken to the pan and add the tomatoes and strips of red pepper. Sprinkle with the paprika and season with salt and pepper. Bring to simmering point, then cover with a lid and cook in the oven for 20 minutes.

Meanwhile, make the cobbler. Sift the flour and baking powder into a large bowl and rub in the butter lightly and quickly with your fingertips, then stir in the grated cheese and thyme. Add the cream or milk and mix with a fork until the dough coheres.

Flour your hands and shape the dough into little scones, about 5cm/ 2 inches in diameter and 1cm/½ inch thick. Plop them on top of the stew, sprinkle over a little extra grated cheese and return to the oven. Cook, uncovered, for a further 40 minutes or until the cobbles have swollen and turned golden and crisp.

Leave to stand for 10 minutes before serving.

> If you are using rabbit, to serve 6 you really need to ask your butcher for an extra couple of legs. Joint the whole rabbit into 2 back legs and split the saddle in two.

Pheasant braised with chicory,
white wine and crème fraîche

This dish works just as well with guinea fowl, and in season the lovely garnet coloured Treviso chicory to offset an otherwise ivory dish. The sauce is sharpened with crème fraîche and lemon juice and the endives sweetened with a little dark sugar. No other vegetable is needed, though you may like to serve it with green beans and mashed potato, or follow it with a green salad.

serves 4

2 tbsp olive oil

55g/2oz unsalted butter

2 jointed pheasants, legs on the bone, breasts whole

sea salt and black pepper

8 heads of pale chicory or Treviso, or half of each

1 onion, peeled and finely chopped

1 level tbsp molasses or dark muscovado sugar

juice of 1 lemon

200ml/7fl oz white wine

240ml/8fl oz crème fraîche

a handful of flat-leaf parsley, finely chopped

Heat the olive oil and butter together in a heavy-bottomed cooking pot. Add the pheasant joints, skin side down, and cook until golden brown, then turn to brown the other side and season with salt. Remove to a plate with a slotted spoon.

Throw the chicory heads into the pot with the onion and sugar and cook for about 5 minutes, turning them to colour all over. Add the lemon juice and return the birds to the pot. Pour in the wine, bring to the boil and allow it to simmer for a few minutes.

Pour in the crème fraîche and season with pepper. Cover the surface with a circle of greaseproof paper, cut to fit (a cartouche), and put the lid on. Cook at a gentle simmer for 30–40 minutes or until the pheasant juices run clear when you insert a skewer through the thickest part of the meat.

Pour the sauce off into a small pan, keeping the meat and chicory hot in the covered pot. Let the sauce bubble for a few minutes to thicken and reduce slightly.

Return the sauce to the pot, throw over the chopped parsley and serve on hot plates.

One pot fish pie
with spinach and leeks

The thing about a good fish pie is that it's not just as good as the cost of the fish you put in it. You can add raw scallops and their coral, shrimps, mussels, clams and prawns, with the more expensive cod, hake or haddock as chief fish, but there is nothing wrong with coley spruced up with a little smoked haddock, a layer of spinach and some leeks and frozen peas. Cut your cloth, or fillet your fish, according to your purse. This really is a one pot wonder too – the base of spinach and the seam of leeks and peas in béchamel allow you to go it alone and not even offer another vegetable unless you want to.

serves 6

900g/2lb coley or other white fish, filleted

180–225g/6–8oz fillet naturally smoked haddock

1 bay leaf

600ml/1 pint full-cream milk, heated

3 or 4 fat leeks, cleaned

55g/2oz unsalted butter

2 tbsp plain flour

1 glass vermouth or white wine

sea salt and black pepper

nutmeg for grating

675g/1½lb or thereabouts spinach, well washed

a few shellfish if your purse can stretch to it, such as cleaned raw scallops (one each) or cooked prawns, mussels or clams (2–3 each)

90–110g/3–4oz frozen peas

2 tbsp chopped dill or half parsley, half dill

for the topping

6 large potatoes, peeled

a little hot milk

several knobs of butter

Preheat the oven to 200°C/Gas 6. Lay the coley and smoked haddock fillets, skin side down, in a large, greased gratin dish. Add the bay leaf and pour over the hot milk. Bake for 10–15 minutes until opaque (or cook gently in a shallow pan on top of the stove for about 10 minutes). In the meantime, boil the potatoes for the topping in the usual way.

While the fish is cooking, finely slice the green part of the leeks and chop the white part into chunks. Melt the butter in a large pan, toss in the leeks (green and white) and stir them around for a few minutes. Scatter in the flour and stir. Once the fish is cooked (it should be by now), pour off the milk into a jug. Gradually stir the fishy milk into the leeks, then add the vermouth or wine, stirring over the heat until the sauce is thickened and smooth.

Season the sauce with salt and pepper and grate over some nutmeg. Cook gently, stirring from time to time. Meanwhile break the fish into large chunks, discarding the skin; set aside on a plate.

Drain the potatoes when they are tender and mash with hot milk and some of the butter.

Cook the spinach, with just the water clinging to the leaves after washing for 2–3 minutes until it has just wilted. Drain, adding the small amount of liquid to the sauce. Spread the spinach over the bottom of the gratin dish and season with salt and pepper.

Scatter the flaked fish over the spinach, along with any extras, like discs of raw scallop or cooked, shelled prawns, mussels or clams. Add the frozen peas to the leek béchamel, stir for a few minutes, then remove from the heat. Add the herbs and adjust the seasoning, then pour the leek béchamel over the fish.

Top with the mashed potato, rough up the surface with a fork and dot with little knobs of butter. Bake for 25 minutes or until browned on top and bubbling at the edges.

Autumn vegetable lasagne

This is not strictly vegetarian but it can be if you want it to be. Nor is it strictly an autumn dish; you just need to tweak the vegetables in the rootier direction if courgettes are past tense and add onion squash, red peppers, celeriac, aubergines or what you will. If the morels are beyond your touch eschew them, likewise the prosciutto, but you need so little of both, and the morels with their bosky funghi liquor contribute so much depth of flavour, that it is worth stretching a financial point if you can. I like the combined forces of pecorino and Parmesan scattered over this dish, but if you only have one or the other don't worry.

serves 4

2 tbsp olive oil

200g/7oz chestnut mushrooms, sliced

20g/¾oz dried sliced morels, soaked in warm water to cover for 30 minutes and drained (optional)

2 tbsp Marsala, or port or Madeira (or red wine if you have a bottle open instead)

900ml/1½ pints Jersey or full-cream milk

1 bay leaf

60g/2oz butter

2 tbsp plain flour

sea salt and black pepper

nutmeg for grating

1 large onion, peeled and finely chopped

2 garlic cloves, peeled and sliced

6 small green or yellow courgettes, cut into small cubes

400g/14oz tin cherry tomatoes

a handful of basil leaves, torn

6 slices prosciutto, sliced into long strips (optional)

1 packet of good-quality dried lasagne (preferably not no-need-to-precook)

60g/2oz each Parmesan and pecorino

Preheat the oven to 200°C/Gas 6. Heat 1 tbsp of the olive oil in a small pan and cook the sliced chestnut mushrooms until they begin to release their juice. Add the morels with their soaking liquor, if using, and the Marsala and simmer for 5 minutes. Remove from the heat.

To make the béchamel sauce: heat the milk with the bay leaf in a pan. Melt the butter in another pan, stir in the flour and cook for a minute or so until you have a biscuit coloured roux, then add a quarter of the hot milk and whisk until smooth. Continue to add the milk a quarter at a time, whisking well. Season and flavour sparingly with nutmeg. Add the liquor from the mushrooms and let the sauce cook gently for a further 15 minutes, stirring from time to time. Adjust the seasoning.

Meanwhile, sauté the onion and garlic in the remaining olive oil with a sprinkle of salt until they begin to soften, then add the courgette cubes and cook until they are al dente. Add the tomatoes and torn basil and simmer the mixture for 10 minutes. Season with pepper.

Add the mushrooms to the béchamel. Heat the prosciutto strips briefly in the pan used to cook the mushrooms with no extra oil, turning until they begin to crisp a little, then add to the mushroom sauce mixture.

Cook the lasagne sheets, according to the packet instructions, until al dente, then drain in a colander.

Spread a little béchamel, avoiding the bits, over the bottom of a large baking dish, then add a layer of lasagne sheets. Cover with half of the remaining béchamel mixture. Add another layer of lasagne, followed by the courgette and tomato mixture. Add a final layer of lasagne and the last of the béchamel mixture. Top with the grated cheese.

Bake for 30 minutes or until golden and bubbling, and a skewer inserted in the centre meets with little resistance from the lasagne. Leave to stand for 10 minutes before serving; this is one of those dishes that seems to stay hotter for longer.

> **If you find the courgette and tomato mixture is rather more than you need for the single seam of brightness through the middle of your lasagne, keep the mixture for a pasta sauce to make a something-from-nothing supper (see page 175).**

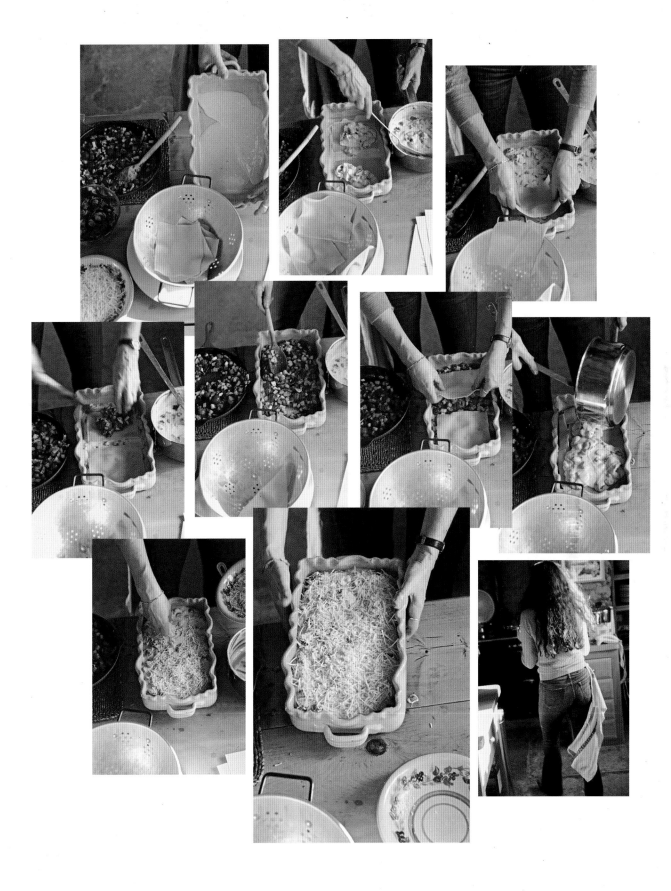

Happy food

A life without treats is unthinkable. Treating ourselves, being spoilt – such unfortunate words for something we all desire and deserve – spoiling the ones we love, is more often than not just cooking or eating the food that makes us happy. It should be guilt-free but it rarely is: pleasure, greed and guilt, are, after all, major contributors to our sense of well-being and wickedness, and are all part of the fun.

When we are broke we need to reward ourselves more than ever, with little luxuries in the absence of large. On high days and holidays, on broken-heart days and midwinter-blues nights, at teatime, on birthdays, on cold sullen rainy days, any days, we need cheering-up, mood-altering substances like chocolate, cream, strawberries, cherries, butter and bread.

Good, home-baked bread straight out of the oven, crisp, caramelly crusted and warm within – slicked with cold salty butter or sweet unsalted French or Italian butter – well, I could happily live on it if I had to choose one food and one alone, though it would be a tough call between bread and potatoes.

A garlicky, creamy dauphinois, or a steaming bowl of smooth-as-silk buttery mash? I'd have to toss a coin between those two. Crisp roast potatoes ruffled with a fork and turned in hot goose fat, the ultimate indulgence. What else? A bitter-sugar topped brûlée, a wobbly pannacotta dotted with vanilla, crème caramel with brittled nuts, or some rich vanilla ice cream with a dark chocolate sauce that seizes, freezes and sets on top of it.

Thinking about food always makes me happy. But it isn't quite enough. It's not all about cream and butter, a lot of it is about simple pleasures, such as a ripe white Italian peach or nectarine, a Gariguette strawberry or dark cherries on a white plate.

As I write this in a cold-snap of winter, drifts of snow against the door, the track to the house impassable, the fruit cage so weighted with last night's snowfall that it has collapsed like the broken hull of a ship dashed on rocks in a storm, I am savouring a bowl of red onion squash gnocchi – starchy and satisfying, slippery with butter and snipped sage, showered in their own snow-storm of Parmesan and Pecorino (see page 168). Pure comfort food that makes me happy. Even the colour is a happy colour. When the gnocchi bob to the surface of the simmering water like miniature lifebuoys, it's as though the sun has just come up.

Thinking about food is so much about remembering the first time a particular dish or ingredient infused you with happiness. If only I could revisit some of those memories, go back to Alba for a bowl of home-made buttered taglierini with grated white truffle and nothing else, with a scent so bewitching it could be the scent of the devil telling me more, more. Yes, food memories are a great source of happiness: the time, the place, the people one ate the particular dish with.

And chocolate: cure-all, seduce-all chocolate. Good chocolate never fails. A chocolate espresso cake, a box of Gerard Coleman's best from L'Artisan du Chocolat, a bag of his salted caramels in cocoa-dusted ganache – one bite and the caramel explodes in your mouth with a final note of salt upon the tongue.

Here are some recipes that I hope will make you happy too. They may bring back memories or inspire new ones.

White chocolate and raspberry truffles

There is almost as much pleasure in skewering these cold raspberries and twirling them in chocolate fondue-style as there is in eating them, but I will leave you to find that out for yourselves. Any child can do it and if you're not in pudding mode, these will please every bit as much.

makes about 30

200g/7oz punnet raspberries

200g/7oz good white chocolate

up to 10g/⅓oz unsalted butter

Put the raspberries on a plate in a single layer in the freezer for 30 minutes.

Melt the chocolate in a double boiler or in a heatproof bowl set over a pan of simmering water, but not touching the water.

Remove the pan from the heat, keeping the melted chocolate over the warm water. Drop a couple of tiny knobs of butter into the chocolate to stop it seizing.

Spike a skewer through a raspberry and dip it into the chocolate until it is enrobed completely. Place the truffle on a foil-lined tray to set. Continue. If the chocolate seems to be hardening, add another few tiny knobs of butter and 1 tsp boiling water to help thin it, stirring both in.

When you have finished, put the tray of truffles in the fridge until the chocolate has completely set.

Chocolate and chestnut terrine

This is the perfect pudding, with a lovely fondant texture to the chocolate and a lighter, creamier chestnut layer to complement it. Nothing complicated, it is so worth making, and much, much easier than the end result suggests. You can make the terrine in advance and keep it in the freezer for a few days if you need to.

Don't use tinned chestnut purée, it always seems to taste tinny. Sierra Rica organic sweet chestnut purée in a jar is wonderful and inexpensive.

serves 8–10

150g/5½oz dark chocolate,
64–72% cocoa solids

150g/5½oz vanilla caster
sugar

125ml/4fl oz water

5 organic large egg yolks

300ml/½ pint double cream

2 tbsp kirsch

250g jar sweet chestnut
purée (I use Sierra Rica
organic)

to finish

dark chocolate, for grating

4–5 chestnuts in syrup, to
finish (optional)

Line a 900g/2lb terrine or loaf tin with cling film, allowing enough overhang to cover the top later. Melt all but 30g/1oz of the chocolate gently in a double boiler or heatproof bowl over a pan of simmering water, making sure the bowl is not touching the water. Once melted, remove the bowl from the pan.

Meanwhile, dissolve the sugar in the water in a heavy-bottomed pan over a medium-low heat. Bring to the boil and simmer for 10 minutes or until you have a syrupy consistency. Do not boil rapidly, otherwise the syrup will reduce too much and over-thicken, leaving it difficult to work into the egg yolks.

While the syrup is simmering, whisk the egg yolks thoroughly using an electric mixer; I do this for 3–4 minutes. Pour the hot syrup in a steady stream onto the egg yolks, then whisk for about 10 minutes or until the mixture has dramatically increased in volume and turned pale, light and fluffy.

Whip the cream in a bowl until it holds in soft folds. Add the kirsch and whisk it in briefly. Empty the sweet chestnut purée into a large bowl and scrape the melted chocolate into another.

Using a large metal spoon or spatula, alternately fold half the whipped cream into the chestnut mixture followed by half the whisked egg and sugar mixture. Do the same with the chocolate mixture.

Scrape the chocolate mixture into the prepared terrine or tin and smooth over the surface with a rubber spatula. Scrape the chestnut mixture lightly and carefully onto the chocolate and smooth over. Cover with the overhanging cling film and put in the freezer for at least 6 hours, or overnight, or for a few days if you are preparing ahead.

Remove from the freezer 20 minutes before serving. Turn the terrine out onto a plate and peel away the cling film. Grate or scrape curls of chocolate over the top and, if you have them, throw some chestnuts in syrup, broken by hand, around the terrine.

Rich chocolate truffle cake

Sometimes one wants rich. A small slice of something utterly dazzling, which for me with chocolate has to be something on the critically-rich list. Yes, there is a lot of chocolate and a lot of cream in this recipe, but a little goes such a long way that this is not a financially out-of-bounds pudding. You don't need to use a very expensive chocolate either. I used Menier and it was decidedly good enough.

Also, since you can make this truffle cake in minutes and it doesn't even have to hit the oven, it is time, cost and energy effective. Not that good chocolate ever needs such an excuse. Just tell yourself there is no butter, flour or sugar in it if you need to feel a modicum of virtue.

serves 10

450g/1lb dark chocolate,
64–74% cocoa solids
(Menier is fine)

600ml/1 pint Jersey or
double cream

cocoa powder for sprinkling
(I use Green and Black's)

Line a 20cm/8 inch cake tin as well as you can with cling film, allowing the edges to drape over the rim so that it won't shoot down into the tin when you pour in the chocolate mixture.

Bash the chocolate into bits and melt in a double boiler or in a large heatproof bowl over a pan of barely simmering water, making sure the bowl is not touching the water. Every so often, stir the chocolate a little as it melts.

In the meantime, warm the cream in a pan, but do not let it get hot. When the chocolate has melted, remove the top of the double boiler or the bowl from the pan and stir in the cream off the heat.

Pour the chocolate and cream mixture into the cake tin and allow it to cool, then put it into the fridge to firm up for 4 hours or so, or until the truffle cake is clearly no longer at all wobbly.

Remove from the fridge and lift the cake out of the tin. Hold an upturned serving plate over the top – a white plate always looks good for a dark chocolate cake – then turn over, so that you have the smooth underside on top. Sprinkle the cake with a thin layer of cocoa powder and return to the fridge.

Remember to take the cake out of the fridge 15 minutes before you intend to eat it. You may like to serve it with cream whipped with a little icing sugar and 1 tbsp cooled, very strong espresso whisked in. Or you may just serve it alone or with a few raspberries on the side.

Baked bitter chocolate custards

I have made this dish from a standing start, as it were, when inviting people to dinner at the last minute and thinking, Help! I must make a pudding. It is pretty much a store-cupboard recipe, and chocolate at that.

A blackberry compote and a home-made blackberry sorbet are happy partners – the warm and cool and chill work well – but equally these custards stand alone perfectly.

serves 4

100g/3½oz dark chocolate

4 tbsp double cream

1 tbsp freshly made strong coffee, cooled to tepid

200ml/⅓ pint Jersey or full-cream milk

4 organic large egg yolks

55g/2oz unrefined caster sugar

Preheat the oven to 150°C/Gas 2. Melt the chocolate with the double cream in a double boiler or a heatproof bowl over a pan of gently simmering water.

As the chocolate melts, stir in the coffee. Remove from the heat and whisk in one-third of the milk.

Whisk the egg yolks in a separate bowl, then whisk in the sugar until the mixture is pale and creamy. Pour in the chocolate mixture and fold together using a spatula until evenly combined.

Pour the chocolate mixture into 4 ramekins, dividing it equally between them. Stand the ramekins in a roasting tin and surround with enough boiling water to come halfway up their sides. Bake for about 25 minutes or until the custards have set.

Remove the ramekins from their bain-marie and let the custards cool to warm before serving.

Date and coffee sponge
with a coffee glaze

Instant gratification is hard to come by without resorting to chocolate, but here is a lovely, quick-to-make cake that I've decided belongs in this chapter because it is a cake with a difference. It can be a pudding too. With its intensely coffee, not-too-sweet crackle top, it is such a delight. Use the winter season's toffee-ish Medjool dates and you can make it taste really special, but any date will do. This is a cake to eat with coffee too.

serves 8–10

180g/6oz butter

1 tbsp freshly ground coffee

5 tbsp boiling water

2 organic large eggs

180g/6oz light muscovado sugar

200g/7oz plain flour

2 level tsp baking powder

125ml/4fl oz full-cream milk

160g/5½oz pitted dates, chopped into quarters

for the glaze

120g/4½oz unrefined icing sugar

20g/¾oz butter, melted, hot

2 tbsp strong coffee (from above)

2–3 tsp boiling water (if needed)

Preheat the oven to 150°C/Gas 2. Grease a 27 x 21cm/11 x 8 inch roasting pan or tin with similar dimensions, about 5cm/2 inches deep.

Melt the butter in a small pan and set aside. Make the coffee with the boiling water, strain and set aside 2 tbsp for the glaze.

Whisk the eggs using an electric mixer. Add the muscovado sugar, flour, baking powder, melted butter, milk and 2 tbsp coffee. Whisk until amalgamated, then fold in the dates by hand. Pour the mixture into the prepared tin and make sure the dates are evenly distributed.

Bake for 30 minutes or until a skewer inserted into the middle comes out clean. Place the tin on a rack to cool the cake slightly while you make the glaze.

For the glaze, tip the icing sugar into a bowl. Melt the butter and, while it is still hot, pour onto the icing sugar, followed by the reserved 2 tbsp coffee. Stir until smooth. The consistency should be thick so that you know the glaze will set as it cools. If it seems too thick, add 2–3 tsp boiling water to thin.

Pour the glaze over the cake in the tin and smooth gently with a palette knife. There will be just enough to cover the cake; this is not a thick icing.

If you can restrain yourself from cutting the first slice until the icing has cooled and set, good for you.

Cardamom and orange crème caramel
with nut brittle

It is often the simplest old jerseys of dishes, the well-worn, tried and tested old favourites that give the most pleasure, either made as they have always been made, or revamped a little with a twist of the new. This is one. It is a real shoestring of a pudding too, and you will always have the ingredients to hand.

Orange and cardamom are perfect bedfellows, and served with more-ish brittle, this is as comforting as anything milky or creamy can be. Satin textured, it slips and slides on the plate and delivers that lovely combination of sweet creaminess and bitter nuttiness. You won't be able to resist breaking off shards of brittle to eat solo either, so consider doubling the quantity.

serves 6

85g/3oz vanilla caster sugar, plus 2 tbsp

1 tbsp cold water

2 organic large eggs, plus 2 extra yolks

1 vanilla pod, split, seeds scraped

600ml/1 pint Jersey or full-cream milk

6 cardamom pods, cracked open to expose the seeds

a few drops of sweet orange oil

finely grated zest of 1 orange

for the nut brittle

30–40g/1–1½oz each pistachios, hazelnuts and almonds

85g/3oz vanilla caster sugar

Preheat the oven to 150°C/Gas 2. Have ready a 20–22cm/8–8½ inch soufflé dish. Gently melt the 85g/3oz sugar in a heavy-bottomed frying pan until it is liquid and has turned a burnished mahogany colour. Just as it starts to bubble, throw in the cold water and instantly pour the caramel into the prepared dish. Tilt and turn the dish so the caramel coats the base and partway up the sides as it sets.

Whisk the eggs, extra yolks, 2 tbsp sugar and vanilla seeds together in a bowl. Slowly heat the milk in a pan with the empty vanilla pod and cracked cardamom pods to just below the boil. Immediately pour it onto the egg and sugar mixture, whisking as you do so. Cover and leave to infuse for 10 minutes.

Strain the mixture onto the caramel base. Place the soufflé dish in a roasting tin and pour in enough boiling water to come two-thirds of the way up the side. Cook in the oven for 1½–2 hours or until you can see the custard has set. It should still be a little wobbly in the middle.

Leave the dish in the bain-marie to cool the crème caramel slowly, then chill in the fridge for a few hours.

For the brittle, chop the nuts very slightly. Scatter the vanilla sugar over the base of a heavy-bottomed pan and heat it to a burnished mahogany colour (as for the caramel). Throw in the nuts, stir for a few seconds, sloshing the caramel over the nuts to cover them completely, then pour onto a greased baking tray and allow to set firm.

To turn the crème caramel out, run a palette knife cautiously around the edge of the dish, place an upturned deep plate – that will hold the liquid caramel – over the top of the dish and invert it carefully. Bash the brittle up a little to serve with the caramel.

Bitter chocolate sorbet

A shot of espresso intensifies this near-black sorbet, which feels rich to the tongue with cocoa, although there isn't a drop of cream in it. I think in its most exuberant state it should be served alongside a pannacotta (such as the one opposite), together with some raspberries, but better a solitary scoop of sorbet than no pudding at all.

serves 6–8

240g/8½oz dark chocolate, 64–72% cocoa solids

2 tbsp cocoa powder (I use Green and Black's)

2 tbsp freshly made espresso, cooled to tepid

210g/7½oz unrefined granulated sugar

600ml/1 pint water

Break up the chocolate and place it in a heatproof bowl with the cocoa powder and espresso.

Put the sugar and water into a heavy-bottomed pan and dissolve over a medium-low heat, stirring. Bring to the boil and then continue to boil the sugar syrup for 5 minutes.

Remove from the heat and pour the sugar syrup over the broken chocolate and cocoa powder, stirring as you do so until the chocolate has completely melted. Allow to cool to tepid.

Pour the mixture into an ice-cream machine if you have one and churn until set, or freeze in a suitable container, whisking every hour for the first 3 hours to break down the ice crystals.

Either serve the sorbet straight away or keep it in a sealed container in the freezer, taking it out about 15 minutes before you wish to serve it to allow it to soften slightly. It really is best eaten within a week.

Piedmont pannacotta

More of that milky, creamy thing that always seems to satisfy, and is cool and elegant, not just nursery pudding-ish. The traditional pannacotta from Piedmont has a burst of pêche de vigne in it. If you do not have any then use an eau de vie from another fruit, such as prune, pear, quetsche, kirsch, raspberry or Marc instead, or just add a nuance of orange flower or rose water if you'd rather. This pudding is all about texture and cool smoothness, so little speckles of vanilla are enough if you want it booze-free and not like a scented bough!

Pannacotta is often served alongside sugared and macerated fresh berries or a fruit compote, depending on the season. A lovely idea but do keep the flavours separate – this is not about raspberry coulis poured over pannacotta.

serves 6

425ml/¾ pint double cream

150ml/¼ pint Jersey or full-cream milk

1 vanilla pod, split, seeds scraped

85–100g/3–3½oz vanilla caster sugar

10g/⅓oz leaf gelatine sheets (see below)

4 tbsp hot water

2–3 tbsp pêche de vigne or other fruit eau de vie (optional)

Oil 6 ramekins, dariole moulds or individual steamed pudding basins, using almond oil or another tasteless oil.

Put the cream, milk, vanilla seeds and empty pod in a heavy-bottomed pan, add the sugar and heat slowly until the sugar dissolves. Simmer gently for a minute, keeping a watchful eye on the pan, then take the pan off the heat. Cover and leave the mixture to infuse as it cools. Remove the vanilla pod.

Soften the gelatine in a shallow dish of cold water for a few minutes, then squeeze out excess water and dissolve in 4 tbsp hot water.

Strain the cream mixture into a bowl, then add 2 tbsp of it to the gelatine, stirring rapidly. Now add the gelatine to the cream mixture, stirring thoroughly to dissolve it. Add the eau de vie or other flavouring, if using, at this point. You want a scent, not an overwhelming taste of alcohol.

Pour the mixture into the oiled dishes and allow to cool. Cover with cling film and chill in the fridge for at least 2 hours or until set.

To serve, run a knife around the edge of each pannacotta and turn out onto individual plates.

Gelatine leaves now vary in size considerably, so weight is the easiest way to measure them. Check the packet instructions for recommended quantities and setting capacities.

General satisfaction

This lovely Victorian nursery pudding is addictive, like a comfort blanket, and delectable in equal measure. And with a name like this, happiness is clearly its heartland. Those old-fashioned sponge fingers, which are a good store-cupboard stand-by for a trifle or syllabub, are made jammy, custardy and meringuey. That's all there is to it.

serves 6

1 level tbsp cornflour

425ml/scant ¾ pint full-cream milk

1 vanilla pod, split, seeds scraped

3 organic large eggs, separated

90g/3oz vanilla caster sugar, plus 3 tbsp

½ x 340g/12oz jar apricot, raspberry or strawberry jam, or blackcurrant jelly

1 tsp water

12–15 savoiardi or sponge fingers

a little oloroso or Palo Cortado sherry, to sprinkle (optional)

Preheat the oven to 180°C/Gas 4. Mix the cornflour with 1 tbsp of the milk.

Pour the rest of the milk into a small, heavy-bottomed pan and add the vanilla seeds, empty pod and blended cornflour. Bring to the boil, stirring, and simmer, still stirring, for a couple of minutes. Remove from the heat.

Whisk the egg yolks in a bowl, then whisk in the hot milk. Return to the pan and whisk over a low heat until the custard thickens and is perfectly smooth; don't let it boil. Remove from the heat and whisk in 2 tbsp sugar. Leave to cool.

Gently melt the jam or jelly with 1 tsp water until runny and pour it over the base of a medium baking dish. Lay the savoiardi on top and sprinkle with a little sherry, as you would for a trifle or tiramisu. Strain the cooled custard through a sieve over the sponge fingers.

Whisk the egg whites until stiff, then whisk in the 90g/3oz sugar, 1 tbsp at a time, to make a firm, shiny meringue. Spoon the meringue over the custard and sprinkle the final spoonful of sugar on top.

Bake on the middle shelf of the oven for about 20 minutes until the meringue is pale gold on top and crisp when you tap it.

Serve warm, with thin cream flavoured with a little sweet orange oil or the grated zest of an orange if you like.

Tiramisu

Pudding snobbery is something I abhor. Yes, a tiramisu is the Italian answer to trifle, but there is nothing intrinsically wrong with that. It may have got something of a bad name from poor factory-made imitations. At best it is a dish of lovely textures and flavours, of hidden depths and subtlety, and when made with the best ingredients, just happens to be one of my favourite puddings.

This particular version combines everything I know that is the secret to happiness. Ignore it if you are a miserabilist, make it the day before you want to eat it if you want untold pleasure.

serves 6

1 organic large egg, plus 3 extra yolks

50ml/2fl oz white wine

50ml/2fl oz Marsala

2 tbsp Amaretto di Saronno (or use Cognac and a few drops of natural almond extract)

90g/3oz unrefined vanilla caster sugar

225g/8oz mascarpone

1 tsp instant espresso coffee powder or 1 tbsp strong black coffee

for the sponge layer

3 small cups espresso coffee or strong black coffee

1½ tbsp vanilla caster sugar

2 tbsp Marsala

175g/6oz savoiardi or sponge fingers, or amaretti biscuits

2 level tbsp dark cocoa powder (I use Green and Black's)

Whisk together the egg, egg yolks, white wine, Marsala and Amaretto in a double boiler or in a bowl set over a pan of simmering water, making sure the bowl is not touching the water. Continue to whisk until the mixture becomes a thick and frothy zabaglione.

Remove from the heat and whisk for another couple of minutes. Shoot in the sugar and let it dissolve. Gently fold in the mascarpone with the coffee powder or liquid until the mixture lightens to a cream.

For the sponge layer, mix together the espresso, sugar and Marsala in a shallow dish. One by one, briefly dip half of the savoiardi into the espresso mixture, on both sides so that they absorb the liquid but do not break up. Immediately lay them, side by side, in a large, shallow serving dish.

Spoon half the zabaglione mixture over the savoiardi. Repeat with another layer of savoiardi, facing them at right angles in the dish to the first layer; this helps the tiramisu to hold together when you serve it.

Cover with the rest of the zabaglione and sift over far more cocoa powder than looks sensible. It needs to well and truly cover the surface, not be a mere dusting. Cover and chill in the fridge, ideally overnight, until ready to serve.

Tartiflette

This is midwinter mountain food, for both on and off the piste, and as close as it gets to comfort and joy. Eat it at the top of the mountain and you will be a little closer to heaven naturally. It is also what your body craves to carry it through the exertions and cold of the afternoon ahead. But don't worry if you're a lowlander, as long as the weather is harsh, the time is right for a tartiflette.

The inimitably creamy, fruity tang of Reblochon, a Savoie cheese that is as brilliant as Comté for cooking with, is what makes this simple dish quite as pleasurable as it is.

serves 4

675g/1½lb potatoes, peeled
sea salt and black pepper
140g/5oz streaky bacon or pancetta
1 medium onion, peeled
60g/2oz butter
150ml/¼ pint warmed white wine
½ Reblochon, 340g/12oz

Preheat the oven to 190°C/Gas 5. Boil the potatoes in salted water until al dente. Meanwhile, cut the bacon into strips and slice the onion into fine rings. Throw the bacon into a pan of boiling water and blanch for a minute, then drain and pat dry. Drain the potatoes and let them cool to the point where you can hold them, then cut them into 1.5cm/½ inch thick slices.

Melt half the butter in a large, heavy-bottomed frying pan and throw in the bacon and onion. Stir to coat in the butter and cook over a gentle heat for 10 minutes or so, until the onion is softened and pale gold. Add the sliced potatoes and the rest of the butter and cook gently, trying not to let the potatoes break up. After 4–5 minutes add the warm wine and continue to cook for 5 minutes.

Scrape the contents of the pan into a greased gratin dish. Cut the Reblochon horizontally through its middle and put each half, rind-side down, on top of the potato mixture. Bake for 20–25 minutes or until the cheese has formed a lovely sticky crust on top.

Leave to stand for 5 minutes before serving with a baguette and a plain green salad with a mustardy dressing.

Ham and Comté cake

You know that feeling before dinner when you just need a little something salty to wake up the taste buds and see you through to dinner, and you don't want to drink without eating. On a recent trip to the Franche-Comté where the great Comté cheese is made, I was told that this 'cake' has become the fashionable French tidbit to serve with an apéritif. It is known simply as 'le cake'. It takes minutes to make and can include any spare ham or bacon rashers, green or black olives, a little thyme, even some stove-top dried tomatoes. A glass of wine – from the Jura to be faithful to the region – is all you'll need with it.

makes 10–12 slices

200g/7oz plain flour

150g/5oz Comté or Gruyère, grated

150g/5oz ham or unsmoked bacon, snipped small

50g/2oz pitted olives, sliced

100g/3½oz butter, melted

2–3 sprigs of thyme, leaves stripped and chopped

3 organic large eggs

1–2 tbsp milk

7g/¼oz sachet fast-action dry yeast

sea salt and black pepper

Preheat the oven to 200°C/Gas 6. Butter a 900g/2lb loaf tin.

Put the flour, cheese, ham, olives, butter, thyme, eggs, milk, yeast and seasoning into a large bowl and mix well. Scrape into the prepared tin.

Bake for 10 minutes, then turn the oven down to 180°C/Gas 4 and bake for a further 20 minutes or until risen and browned. Insert a skewer into the centre to check that it is cooked through; it might need a few minutes longer. There may be some bubbling butter on top of the cake at this stage. If so, just pour some of it away; the rest will be reabsorbed into the cake as it cools.

Leave in the tin on a wire rack to cool for 20 minutes, then turn out and eat warm. Any leftover cake will keep well for a few days wrapped in greaseproof paper and foil. Just cut off the outside slice, which may have dried a little, each time.

Use your loaf

I am the worst culprit. I argue that throwing bread to the birds is not wasting it. I cut my crust to suit my cloth, which inevitably results in end bits and heels, cut-off crusts and leftover slices. Sometimes I make bread for the sheer pleasure of making it, not because I need it. Need doesn't come into it. I window-shop a good loaf in the way some people window-shop for clothes. If I spy a new baker, some particularly beautiful, distinguished-looking bread, if I get the scent of good dough, I will buy two, three, four loaves; to try them all. Reality sets in when I get home. It goes against the grain to cut a slice from each one of them. Now which do I freeze and which do I tuck into now?

A good loaf has both beauty and irresistibility. I find I can never deny myself, and that goes for brioches and croissants too. I am on a continuous search for the best loaf, the best crust, the lightest, egg-rich, yeastiest brioche that just pulls away when you tear it, that is warm enough and sweet enough and dry crusted to perfection. Pull off its little beret first and eat it whole with cold French escure butter.

And then there is the croissant: flaky, buttery yet not greasy, substantial yet ethereal. Maybe a second one. Maybe butter on top too – though the French would never do it. And the search for the best apricot jam, for that is the best match for both, the croissant and the brioche. I can't resist a good loaf. Or brioche. Or croissant.

I am determined to mend my ways: to eat up my crusts and cook and freeze to the last stray slice. To bake rolls more often, so I can freeze, then unfreeze them – one by one, or two by two. To make smaller loaves, to slice and freeze, to turn to crumb or chunk and leave not even the mouthful my father would always leave on the edge of his plate. 'Papa, why have you left that little bit of bread?' I always asked, and the answer was always the same, 'For the little people.' An Irish expression for the fairies, it's a part

of my childhood memory of food and will live with me always.

Bread is the easiest and most satisfying of foods to use up, even, or rather particularly, when it is stale. It takes on a new life, new hope, new invention when stale, and there aren't many things in life one can say that about. It is possibly the most versatile ingredient in the world, when fresh, when stale, whenever. We can make salads, soups and stuffings with it, and sauces for fish, chicken and vegetables. We can make pain perdu and the best traditional English puddings. We can bake bread and fry bread, dry bread and dunk bread. We can do much the same with stale brioche and croissants – we just need a pinch of spice and imagination, of fruit and eggs and milk and sugar, and our daily bread is reincarnate.

If there is any better, more evocative scent in the world than that of bread baking, bread cooling – yeasty, crusty, savoury, sweet – I have yet to smell it. I promise I will not waste bread.

Making bread

Lay the myth to rest. Practice makes perfect, yes, but anyone can make bread and the time involved is about waiting, not working, not difficulty. The end result is so worth it in my book. And bread is easy to make in bulk and freeze if you can get into the groove. I buy Shipton Mill organic flour in bulk and get my fresh yeast for next to nothing from the bread counter at any supermarket in-store bakery.

These loaves call for around 10 minutes of good arm-wrestling work to stretch the gluten, but getting the dough started the night before takes as long as it takes to fill a hot water bottle and really isn't any more complicated. The slow fermentation means that the flavour and the digestibility of this bread are unequalled by any quick-rise method.

the night before

130ml/4½fl oz nearly hot water (between hot and tepid)

a piece of fresh yeast, the size of a large walnut

150g/5½oz stoneground wholewheat bread flour

the next stage

450g/1lb wholewheat or half wholewheat, half white bread flour

50g/2oz organic plain white flour

a handful of toasted bran and wheatgerm (from Shipton Mill), optional

2 tsp sea salt

1 tbsp organic blackstrap molasses

1 tbsp organic malt syrup (if you haven't any, use 2 tbsp molasses)

1 tbsp olive oil

270–300ml/9–10fl oz nearly hot water (between hot and tepid)

semolina to sprinkle

beaten egg to glaze

1 tbsp each poppy, sunflower and sesame seeds, or any combination (optional)

The night before, or at least 12 hours ahead, put the nearly hot water into a jug and add the yeast. Agitate with a fork until it has dissolved.

Put the flour into a bowl, pour on the warm, yeasty liquor and mix with a fork until combined; the bowl needs to be big enough for the dough to treble in volume. Cover the bowl with cling film and leave at room temperature. Go to bed!

The next day, tip the flours and wheatgerm mix into a really large bowl and add the sea salt, molasses, malt syrup and olive oil. Scrape the previous night's sticky dough on top. Add 270ml/9fl oz nearly hot water at this stage and work with your fingers until the mixture coheres. You will probably need to add more of the warm water.

Tip the dough onto a lightly floured surface and work, kneading with your fingers and occasionally stretching out the dough – unfurling it with the heel of your hand then rolling it back towards you. Keep this up for 10 minutes, then put the dough back into the large bowl and cover the bowl with a damp tea-towel. Leave the dough to rise until it has doubled in size; this will take an hour or so.

Next, scatter semolina evenly over a large baking sheet. Either divide the dough into a dozen or so rolls, or into two small loaves or one large loaf, and place on the baking sheet, spacing rolls apart. Cover with a huge plastic bag, forming a tent that doesn't touch the dough.

Preheat the oven to 220°C/Gas 7. Leave the dough to rise in a warm place, perhaps near the oven, for 15–20 minutes.

Uncover the dough and brush with egg glaze. Throw some seeds or extra semolina on top if you feel like it. Place on a higher oven shelf, with enough ceiling space for the dough to rise. Bake in the oven for

about 40 minutes for a single loaf, but check at 30 minutes, and again at 35 minutes if the crust is looking brown. A brace of loaves should be checked at 25 minutes but will probably take 30 minutes. Rolls will only need 15–20 minutes. To test, tap the underside with your knuckles: the bread will sound hollow if it is cooked through. Immediately remove to a wire rack to cool.

Resist scoffing until it is only just warm, as still-steaming bread will make the interior crumb damp. Holding back really is the most difficult part of the whole process.

If for any reason you decide not to bake the dough on the day, after kneading you may hold it in the fridge overnight again, in a covered bowl. Then take it out of the fridge and give it 2 hours to rise.

Pa amb oli, pa amb tomàquet

Literally bread and oil, bread and tomato. My old schoolfriend Tomas Graves, son of the poet Robert, wrote a whole book about the subject, *Bread and Oil, Majorcan Culture's Last Stand*. Tomas grew up and still lives in Majorca. The Catalonians call the dish *Pa amb tomàquet* – they don't mention the oil. You need – simply – good bread, good olive oil, sea salt and garlic to taste, and good tomatoes.

The tomato is sometimes just squashed and rubbed onto the bread after the garlic and olive oil, or sometimes placed on top in chunks or slices. The wet tomato juice is the whole idea, however much you rail against the British idea of soggy buttered tomato sandwiches. This is made with good country bread, ideally cooked in a wood-fired oven, so a day old, a few days old, no matter, it is still a good loaf, the lubrication is what this dish is all about.

You may add a few anchovies or olives, you may lightly toast the bread as in Italian bruschetta before the rubbing commences and then sprinkle oregano over the tomato if you like. This way of not wasting crumb or crust is a natural accompaniment to a drink, a soup, or a starter in its own right. Salt it at the end, onto the tomato. Children in Majorca often sugar it.

Summer panzanella

If I were to say 'stale bread salad' would you turn the page and think no, how unappealing?
'Stale' has these dreary, derogatory connotations, Shakespearean even, as Hamlet cries,

> *'How weary, stale, flat, and unprofitable*
> *Seem to me all the uses of this world.'*

Yet stale is good. All the uses of the loaf are nothing if not profitable and delicious when
stale and weary – and sometimes even flat. Have you ever dampened and griddled stale pita
bread and torn it into a Greek salad, sprinkling it with good, young feisty olive oil as you go?
Perhaps added a little halloumi, also griddled? What a lunch.

serves 6

4 best large, ripe tomatoes

1 large cucumber

1 red onion, peeled, halved and sliced into fine half moons

4–5 tbsp really good fruity, peppery olive oil

sea salt and black pepper

1 small, dried, hottish chilli, deseeded and finely chopped

6 thick slices stale, good country bread, crusts removed

2–3 tbsp iced water

2 tbsp aged red wine vinegar

a small handful of basil leaves, torn

1 level tbsp tiny capers, rinsed and drained

To peel the tomatoes, first spike them with the tip of a knife, then immerse in a bowl of boiling hot water for 30 seconds to loosen the skins. Immediately drain and refresh under cold water – you don't want them to cook. Prise out the core with the tip of a small knife, then peel away the skin. Halve and deseed the tomatoes, then chop chunkily, saving the juices.

Peel the cucumber, quarter lengthways and scoop out the seeds with a teaspoon. Cut the cucumber into batons.

Combine the tomatoes, cucumber and onion in a large bowl and toss together with your hands. Add 4 tbsp fruity olive oil to start with and scatter over the dried chilli. Toss again, adding a touch more oil if you think it is needed, then leave for an hour or so to let the flavours get acquainted with each other.

In the meantime, preheat the oven to 160°C/Gas 3. Lay the slices of bread on a baking sheet and toast them in the oven until pale golden and crisp, turning halfway through; this may take up to 30 minutes. Dampen them a little with the tomato juice. Put a slice of toast on each serving plate, or arrange them on a large platter.

Just before serving, pour 2–3 tbsp iced water and the wine vinegar over the salad in the bowl and toss well. Pile on top of the toasted bread and scatter over the torn basil and capers.

Winter panzanella

Here is the Italian version. My winter Italian version, because the turn of the year is the time for lovely garnet and cream-leaved Treviso chicory and pale, bitter endives, which add so much colour and flavour to a winter dish. And in winter, cooked and raw can work together so well. Salads are not always appealing in the cold months. Add bread, add something cooked, and you will find yourself seduced.

serves 4

1 red pepper, or use good roasted piquillo peppers from a jar (Navarrico wood-roasted are ideal)

1 small red onion, peeled

2 heads of Treviso (red chicory)

1 Belgian endive

1 very thick slice stale, good white country bread, crusts removed

a handful of cherry tomatoes or stove-top dried tomatoes (see page 161), halved

3–4 anchovies, chopped

1 tbsp capers, rinsed and drained

a handful of good olives (tiny black Taggiasca or giant green Mammuth are my favourites here), pitted and sliced

6–8 basil or sage leaves

for the dressing

a splash of olive oil

a drizzle of red wine vinegar

black pepper

If using a fresh red pepper, char it all over under a hot grill, or by holding it with a pair of tongs over a gas burner, then place in a bowl, cover with cling film and leave for 5 minutes or so (the steam will loosen the skins). Peel while still warm, then remove the core and seeds. Cut the roasted pepper into broad strips.

Slice the red onion as thinly as you can, preferably using a mandolin. Halve the Treviso and endive vertically and chop a few chunks from their base at the same time. Throw everything into a large, colourful salad bowl as you go.

Tear the bread into large chunks and lightly run cold water over each chunk, then squeeze it out inefficiently so that it is still damp as you toss it into the bowl. Add the tomatoes, roasted red pepper, anchovies, capers and olives, and some torn basil or sage leaves.

Dress the salad sharply. I add the olive oil first and then the wine vinegar, holding my thumb across the open mouth of the vinegar bottle. Salt is unnecessary with anchovies, capers and olives, but a scrunch of pepper is good. Toss the salad with your hands please, it seems to help the flavours mingle and marry.

Best served 30 minutes or so after making – after another toss and taste and adjustment of oil and red wine vinegar if necessary.

Fried mozzarella sandwich

Mozzarella in carozza, or 'mozzarella in a carriage' is a classic snack but, as such, should not be the victim of poor ingredients, inferior bread and mozzarella. A ball of fresh mozzarella di bufala campana is, to my mind, essential for this dish. As is good country bread or ciabatta, eggs and olive oil. Enough said. I sometimes accompany mine with tomato chilli jam (see page 162), which I'm sure Campanians would consider sacrilegious.

serves 4

8 slices good country bread

a 400g/14oz mozzarella di bufala campana, sliced

sea salt and black pepper

225ml/7fl oz full-cream milk

2 organic large eggs

a handful of plain flour

olive oil for shallow-frying

Sandwich the bread slices together in pairs with the mozzarella slices, dividing the cheese equally and seasoning with salt and pepper before you close them.

Pour the milk into a shallow bowl that you can sink the sandwiches into flat. Beat the eggs with some seasoning in another similar bowl. Throw a handful of flour onto a large plate and spread it evenly.

Pour a 1cm/½ inch depth of olive oil into a frying pan, large enough to take a couple of the sandwiches, and heat over a medium-high heat until hot but not smoking.

Meanwhile, dip two of the sandwiches into the milk briefly, then into the flour, shaking off any excess, and then into the egg mixture, again letting any excess drip back into the bowl.

Fry the sandwiches in the hot oil until they are golden brown on both sides, turning them once. Remove and drain on kitchen paper; keep warm while you fry the other two. Serve at once.

Racing eggs

My cousin Deborah and I share a greed, fascination and love of good food, originally inspired by the wonderful cooking we enjoyed at our mutual grandparents' home. We cook similarly, though often dissimilar things, so it's always brilliant to swap notes and ideas. Last year she invited me to the races at Cheltenham. Being Deborah, nothing was ready made for the picnic. Even if you have no interest in horses, you can bet this is a recipe that will delight all ages on a picnic. I couldn't stop eating them.

makes 12

2 slices stale, white or brown bread, crusts removed

1 tsp chopped thyme leaves

1 tbsp finely chopped flat-leaf parsley

12 quail's eggs

225g/8oz good quality pork sausage meat

2 spring onions, finely chopped

3 tsp snipped chives

2 organic large (hen's) eggs

sea salt and black pepper

a handful of seasoned flour

sunflower or groundnut oil for frying

Preheat the oven to 150°C/Gas 2. Blitz the bread with the thyme and parsley in a blender to fine crumbs, then spread out on a baking tray and dry in the low oven for about 15 minutes.

Put the quail's eggs in a small pan of cold water, bring up to the boil and then simmer for just 3 minutes to hard-boil them. Drain and cool immediately under cold running water, then shell them carefully.

Mix the sausage meat with the spring onions, chives and 1 beaten egg. Season, remembering that sausage meat is salty. Divide into 12 equal pieces. Scatter the seasoned flour on a plate.

Roll a quail's egg in the flour, shaking off any excess. Flatten a piece of sausage meat with your hands and wrap it around the egg to enclose it completely. Repeat with the rest of the quail's eggs.

Beat the remaining egg on a plate and tip the herbed breadcrumbs onto another plate. Dip the sausage-coated eggs first into the beaten egg mixture, then into the herbed crumbs to coat them thoroughly and evenly. Set aside on a plate.

Heat a 4cm/1½ inch depth of oil in a large, heavy-bottomed frying pan to 180°C or until a cube of bread dropped into the oil turns golden brown and fizzles in less than a minute. Lower the eggs into the oil and fry, turning carefully and frequently, for 3–4 minutes until browned. Drain on crumpled kitchen paper and eat just warm or cold.

Soup with bread, or bread with soup

Recently, I have started making a different soup almost every day with whatever I've got hanging around, not always relying on stock. Strong, vibrant flavours can come from herbs and spices, from roasting vegetables, rather than cooking them in water, from adding garlic, cheese, a sharp cooking apple. It's amazing quite how big and bold a potage you can build with really very little.

One day I roasted carrot, parsnip and garlic in olive oil with thyme and liquidised them with water. Another day I used up a slightly sad-looking cauliflower by roasting it with red onion, blitzing again with water and finishing the soup with smoked paprika and saffron, dunking in a little yoghurt at the end.

I've made carrot soup with a baked apple tossed in and a crumble of salt blue cheese to sharpen the sweetness. And broccoli soup, heavy on the onion, made with half creamy milk, half water, with strong Cheddar grated in at the blitzing stage.

One outstanding soup came from a fried leek, onion and potato base, to which I added red chilli, lemongrass, garlic, coriander and half a block of creamed coconut with hot water. Roasted and raw can work magic together too, as in the beetroot soup on page 106.

Often when I have leftover pulses, I make a 'soffrito' of chopped onion, garlic, celery and celery leaves, blitz half with water, leaving the rest chunky, and sprinkle with olive oil, Parmesan and parsley to finish. When the cupboard is all but bare, I will forge a garbure of Savoy cabbage and potato with no more added to it than water, seasoning and the puréed cloves from a poached head of garlic.

I find using bread or potato as a thickener in a soup gives it better body and flavour than flour. Sometimes I will throw a cold, baked potato into what otherwise would be a slightly gutless soup, or I add a spoonful of chestnut purée, or purée some of the beans if it is a beany soup. I want floury and thickened, without the soup tasting floury and thickened, and this is the way to do it.

Think of the summery bread-based Spanish soups like gazpacho (see page 109) – cooling, refreshing and packed full of raw flavour.

The more I make soup, the less I resort to enriching with cream and butter. I prefer the simple, strong earthy taste and texture of the basic ingredients to speak for themselves.

Pancotto or bread soup

All over Italy people make this soup with good Pugliese or country bread, so that the result is not gluey. I love this cuisine that salutes the loaf and uses crumb and crust for soups and pastas. Anna Del Conte, the great Italian food writer, says there are as many versions of this as there are cooks. This is one of hers.

serves 4

4 slices stale, good country bread, crusts removed

5 tbsp best extra-virgin olive oil

½ tsp crushed dried chillies

3 garlic cloves, peeled and chopped

2 tbsp chopped flat-leaf parsley

1.5 litres/2¾ pints hot chicken stock

sea salt and black pepper

freshly grated pecorino to serve

Tear the bread into small pieces and blitz in a food processor for a few seconds or chop coarsely.

Put the olive oil, dried chillies, garlic and parsley into a heavy-bottomed pan and sauté for 30 seconds. Add the bread and cook, stirring frequently, for 3–4 minutes until it begins to turn pale brown. Add the hot stock, then cover and simmer for 30 minutes.

Taste the soup and adjust the seasoning if necessary. Serve with a bowl of grated pecorino cheese for sprinkling on top.

Mushroom soup with spices and bread

Use portobello, crimini or chestnut mushrooms here as they are flavoursome enough to hold their own and define the soup. Wholemeal bread is used to add body. If you are using water rather than stock, you really need to include the leek and garlic for flavour.

serves 4

1–2 tbsp olive oil

1 small red or white onion, peeled and finely chopped

2 sprigs of thyme, leaves stripped and chopped

1 leek, green and white parts, cleaned and chopped (optional)

1 garlic clove, peeled and sliced (optional)

sea salt and black pepper

450g/1lb mushrooms, cleaned and sliced

½–1 tsp ground ginger

3–4 juniper berries, slightly crushed with the back of a knife

3–4 tbsp sherry, Marsala, Madeira or red wine, depending on taste and what you have

about 1.1 litres/scant 2 pints hot chicken stock or water

1 thick slice stale wholemeal bread, crusts removed and torn into chunks

Heat the olive oil in a large, heavy-bottomed pan and add the onion and thyme, along with the leek and garlic, if using them. Sprinkle over a little salt and fry gently until the onion has begun to soften.

Add the mushrooms and stir. Sprinkle over ½ tsp ground ginger and the bruised juniper berries. Sauté over a medium heat until the mushrooms have first become dry and then begun to release their juices. At this stage, add the alcohol and let it bubble and become absorbed into the mushroom liquor. After 3–4 minutes add the hot stock or water and bring to the boil.

Cover with a lid, turn down to a simmer and cook gently for about 10 minutes, by which time the mushrooms should have softened enough. Remove from the heat, season and taste. The ginger should give warmth but not be too obtrusive. Add a little more if you need to.

Using a blender, liquidise ladlefuls of the soup with chunks of bread until smooth. Keep some soup and sliced mushrooms back to add bite and texture. Stir the puréed soup back into the pan. Taste and adjust the seasoning. The soup should not be stand-a-spoon-in-it thick, but it should have body.

Roasted and raw beetroot soup with rye

The sweet earthiness of beetroot with its brilliant hue is such a great thing in the dark night of the soul-food winter. Splash it garishly into soups and citrussy, goat's or sheep's cheese salads. It works roasted whole or cut into chunks, or grated raw.

This is my latest discovery: deep, dark rye marrying with the intense flavour of roasted beetroot and the colour and crunch of the raw. A blodge of yoghurt and a sprinkle of chopped tarragon or dill and you're there. Roast the beetroot ahead and the soup takes no time to make.

serves 4

4–5 medium beetroot, cleaned and trimmed, their whiskers left on

1 tbsp olive oil

1 small red or white onion, peeled and finely chopped

1 small garlic clove, peeled and finely chopped

sea salt and black pepper

1.2 litres/2 pints hot chicken stock or water

1 thick slice stale, good black rye bread, crust removed

a little good live yoghurt to finish

1 tsp finely chopped tarragon or dill

Preheat the oven to 200°C/Gas 6. Wrap each beetroot separately and tightly in a piece of foil, except for the one you are going to grate in raw at the end. Roast in the oven for about an hour until cooked. To check, unwrap and pierce with a skewer through to the centre; it should meet with little resistance. Peel the beetroot as soon as they are not too hot to handle and cut them into chunks.

Meanwhile, heat the olive oil in a large, heavy-bottomed pan and add the onion and garlic. Season with a little salt and sauté over a medium heat until softened.

Add the roasted beetroot chunks, followed by the hot stock or water. Bring to a simmer and cook gently for no more than 5 minutes without a lid. You want this part of the cooking process over as quickly as possible so that the beetroot retains its vibrant colour.

Remove from the heat, season with black pepper and add the rye bread. Using a blender, purée the soup in batches. The texture should be thick, yet not too thick. If in doubt, add another ladle of hot stock to thin the soup down a bit. Check the seasoning.

Grate the remaining beetroot coarsely. Pour the soup into warm soup plates and spoon the grated beetroot into the middle. Top with a spoonful of yoghurt and a sprinkle of chopped tarragon or dill.

Gazpacho

This soup predates Roman times and there are said to be as many recipes for it as there are pestles and mortars. It is traditionally accompanied with little bowls of chopped egg, peppers, olives, onion and jamón, for everyone to scatter over their bowls what they will.

If you have time, make the gazpacho the night before and keep it in the fridge overnight for the flavours to develop. If you make it at the last minute, you can put it in the freezer for 30 minutes to chill it quickly.

serves 6

450g/1lb ripe, flavourful tomatoes, or organic tinned tomatoes if you can't get good fresh ones

1 cucumber

2 slices stale, good white country bread, crusts removed

1 small onion, peeled and cut into chunks

2 garlic cloves, peeled and chopped

2 tbsp good peppery olive oil

sea salt and cayenne pepper

1½ red peppers, quartered, cored and deseeded

2 tbsp sherry vinegar

600–850ml/1–1⅓ pints ice-cold water

Roughly chop the tomatoes if you are using fresh ones, skin on, seeds left in. Peel the cucumber, quarter lengthways and scoop out the seeds with a teaspoon, then cut into big chunks.

Hold the bread under the cold tap, then squeeze out the water gently and plop the chunks into the food processor with the onion, garlic, olive oil, 1 tsp salt and a knife tip of cayenne. Blitz briefly to a pulp.

Add the cucumber, red peppers, sherry vinegar and tomatoes and blitz to a coarse rather than a puréed texture. Pour the mixture into a large bowl, then cover and chill for several hours or overnight in the fridge, or quickly in the freezer.

Just before serving, dilute the soup with the ice-cold water, stirring and tasting until you have the flavour and texture you like. Adjust the seasoning and serve in tall glasses or soup bowls.

Spanish chicken
with a saffron and almond sauce

This lovely Moorish dish has been made over the centuries in Spain, but only recently discovered by me. It is so good I cooked it for everyone who came to stay last summer in Ireland, but it tastes just as good in the winter, the sauce thickened with fried bread perhaps a little more than for the summer version. A heap of saffron rice or some new potatoes, the choice is yours, and something green besides. The colour and texture of the sauce may not be beauteous, but please overlook that fact and judge it on flavour alone.

serves 6

1 large chicken, about
2–2.5kg/4½–5½lb, jointed
into 8 pieces (see below)

250ml/8½fl oz hot chicken
stock

36 or so whole, blanched
Marcona almonds

good pinch of saffron
stamens

2–3 tbsp olive oil

3 garlic cloves, peeled and
finely sliced

1 thick slice stale, good
bread, crusts removed

sea salt and black pepper

a suspicion of nutmeg

2 cloves, crushed

125ml/4fl oz fino sherry

a sprig of bay leaves

4 sprigs of thyme, leaves
stripped

1 tbsp flat-leaf parsley

spritz of lemon juice

Have the chicken joints and stock ready. Preheat the oven to 150°C/ Gas 2. Scatter the almonds on a small baking tray and toast in the oven for 5–10 minutes until golden, keeping an attentive eye on them as nothing browns faster than nuts. Discard any deep brown ones, as they will taste bitter and burnt. Set aside.

Soak the saffron stamens in a ladleful of the hot chicken stock in a small bowl.

Heat 2 tbsp olive oil and the garlic slices gently in a large, heavy-bottomed frying pan until hot; do not let the garlic brown. Remove it with a slotted spoon when the oil is hot and set it aside on a plate. Fry the bread in the garlicky oil on both sides until crisp and browned and then remove it to the garlic plate.

Season the pieces of chicken well and sprinkle with a little freshly grated nutmeg and the crushed cloves. Add a little extra olive oil to the pan if you need to and brown the chicken pieces on all sides. This will take about 20 minutes. Remove the browned chicken to a plate.

Add the chicken stock (not the infused saffron stock) to the frying pan with the sherry and scrape up the sediment with a wooden spoon to deglaze the pan. Let the liquids bubble together for a few minutes, then return the chicken to the pan. Add the bay and thyme leaves, crushing them between your fingers. Cover with the lid and simmer for a further 10 minutes.

Blitz the toasted almonds in a blender or food processor until the coarse side of ground. Tear the fried bread into pieces and add to the nuts with the fried garlic, parsley and saffron-infused chicken stock. Blitz to a purée.

Scrape this mixture into the chicken pan and stir to amalgamate with the juices. If it looks very thick, add a little more hot chicken stock. Taste and adjust the seasoning and add a spritz of lemon juice. Taste again – you may need a little more lemon juice – then serve.

I cut the chicken legs and breasts in half to give 8 pieces, saving the wings for another dish (see page 10), or to make stock along with the carcass (see page 14).

Chargrilled broccoli with Romesco

Romesco sauce is great with firm-fleshed white fish or a Spanish tortilla (see page 169). It is also good with char-grilled broccoli, the ordinary or the purple sprouting kind. It gives oomph to anything that needs a strong, hot partner to jazz it up a little. You may make it with just almonds or hazelnuts if that's all you have.

If you don't have a griddle, I'm afraid you won't achieve the chargrilled flavour, but you can finish off the broccoli after blanching it by roasting it in a hot oven with the oil, chilli and garlic. Still good, just different.

serves 4

2 heads of broccoli, broken into florets, or a packet each of purple and green tender stemmed broccoli

3–4 tbsp good, fruity olive oil

1 green chilli, finely chopped, or 1 tsp dried red chilli flakes

1 garlic clove, peeled and sliced

sea salt and black pepper

for the Romesco

30g/1oz blanched Marcona almonds

4 tbsp good, fruity olive oil

2 garlic cloves, peeled and finely chopped

1 thick slice stale, good brown or white bread, crusts removed

225g/8oz tin plum or cherry tomatoes

1 red chilli, deseeded and finely chopped, or ¼–½ tsp cayenne pepper to taste

30g/1oz whole roasted hazelnuts

2 tbsp red wine vinegar

4 tbsp fino sherry

First make the Romesco. Preheat the oven to 150°C/Gas 2. Scatter the almonds on a small baking tray and toast in the oven for 5–10 minutes until golden, keeping a close eye on them as they will colour quickly.

Slowly heat 2 tbsp olive oil in a pan with the chopped garlic; when hot, remove the garlic with a slotted spoon and reserve. Fry the bread briefly on both sides in the garlicky oil until crisp and brown, then remove to the garlic plate.

Add another 2 tbsp olive oil to the pan and tip in the tomatoes with the chopped chilli or cayenne (start with ¼ tsp and add more if needed). Cook down until jammily thick, about 20 minutes. Remove from the heat and set aside to cool.

Grind the hazelnuts and almonds together in a food processor. Tear the bread into chunks and add to the processor with the fried garlic, wine vinegar and sherry. Blitz together. Add the cooled tomato sauce and blitz to a coarse paste.

To cook the broccoli, throw the florets into a large pan of rapidly boiling, salted water and blanch for 2 minutes. Immediately turn into a colander and refresh with cold water to arrest the cooking process and retain the colour. Drain well.

Heat up the griddle. Dry the broccoli florets with kitchen paper, then put them into a bowl. Pour over 2 tbsp olive oil and toss with your hands to coat the florets, then sprinkle over the chilli.

When the griddle is really hot, lay the florets on it, leaving room in between to use the tongs. Turn them once they have scorch marks. Spike the stalks with a skewer to check when they are tender.

Meanwhile, heat another 1 or 2 tbsp olive oil very, very slowly in a small pan with the garlic. Remove from the heat the moment it is hot.

Tip the broccoli into a serving bowl, pour the warm garlicky oil over and season. Serve at once, with the Romesco sauce.

Provençal breadcrumbs

Store these breadcrumbs in an airtight container and you'll have a lovely gratin top at your fingertips for stuffed baked courgettes, aubergines, peppers or tomatoes, or for sprinkling over prosciutto-wrapped leeks, asparagus or fennel baked in a béchamel sauce, scattering grated Parmesan over the crumb before gratinéeing. You can also keep these herbed crumbs in the freezer in a Ziplock bag and sprinkle them over things from frozen.

I add Parmesan, Gruyère and Cheddar to Provençal breadcrumbs to top macaroni cheese, or just Parmesan to the crumbs to finish a pasta bake.

Or you can mix finely chopped olives and anchovies into the herby crumbs, fry them all together in extra olive oil and butter and toss them into pasta with some crème fraîche and stove-top dried tomatoes (see page 161) for supper. A dry chilli crumbled in peps up the heat.

You may just want to fry the herbed crumbs in olive oil and scatter them over broccoli or cauliflower, or Brussels sprouts if you are serving game.

100g/3½oz stale, good brown or white bread

a bunch of flat-leaf parsley

4 sprigs of thyme

4 sprigs of savory

1 sprig of rosemary

2–3 garlic cloves, peeled and roughly chopped

2 tbsp good olive oil

sea salt and black pepper

Preheat the oven to 150°C/Gas 2. Lay the bread slices out on a large baking sheet and place in the oven for 5–10 minutes to dry out. Alternatively you can dry old bread in the warming oven of an Aga, or conventional warming oven. Tear the dry bread into chunks.

Strip all the herb leaves from their stems and place them in a food processor with the garlic. Blitz to chop the herbs finely. Throw in the bread and blitz to a coarse crumb texture. Tip into a bowl.

Add the olive oil and seasoning, toss to coat and tip into a bag or an airtight container.

Crumbs to coat fish

Blitz a good handful of basil leaves with 2 garlic cloves and 50ml/ 2fl oz fruity olive oil in a food processor, then mix with about 50g/2oz dry stale breadcrumbs, the grated zest and juice of a lemon, 2 skinned, deseeded, finely chopped large tomatoes, and some salt and pepper.

You may either coat egged fillets of plaice or dabs with this or spread a little on top of steamed mussels or clams sitting on their half-shells and then grill them until browned and sizzling.

Spaghetti with broccoli,
chilli and fried breadcrumbs

Pasta and breadcrumbs may not immediately seem appealing, but 'cucina povera' is a fact of life in Italy whether you are impoverished or rich. In poorer regions, such as Puglia and much of southern Italy, people eat the same food whatever their income, which says a lot about both the people and the food, and all to the good. If you can't afford Parmesan, pecorino or meat, your pasta can still be dressed in its best with fried breadcrumbs and a few flavourings.

This dish is good with purple sprouting or florets of ordinary broccoli. You may, or may not wish to add a little anchovy and some pine nuts.

serves 4

450g/1lb broccoli or purple sprouting

450g/1lb wholewheat or ordinary spaghetti

salt

4–5 tbsp best olive oil

3 garlic cloves, peeled and finely sliced

2 tsp dried chilli flakes or 1 dried kashmiri chilli, crumbled

1 thick slice stale, good brown or white bread, crusts removed and blitzed to crumbs

4 anchovies, finely chopped (optional)

25g/1oz pine nuts (optional)

Trim the broccoli and break into florets as necessary. I also use the parts of the stalk that aren't tough, peeling and slicing them into discs.

Add the spaghetti to a pan of well-salted boiling water and cook until al dente.

Meanwhile, very gently warm 2 tbsp olive oil in a large frying pan with the sliced garlic and chilli.

In another frying pan, heat 2–3 tbsp olive oil. When hot, throw in the breadcrumbs and stir to coat. Turn the heat down and keep shifting the crumbs around in the pan until they are golden and crunchy; they must not darken.

In the meantime, throw the broccoli into a pan of fast-boiling water and cook for 3 minutes or until just tender.

Add the anchovies and pine nuts to the garlic and chilli pan if you are using them. Drain the broccoli, refresh under cold water and throw into the pan too, stirring to mix with the other ingredients. You may need a little more oil at this stage.

Drain the pasta, retaining a little water and chute it into the garlic, chilli and broccoli. Toss to combine, then throw in the crumbs and turn to coat. Serve from the pan.

Rhubarb brioche
and butter pudding

There are few things more keenly worked and reinvented than the great bread and butter pudding. My allegiance to brioche and butter pudding with an apricot glaze, bread and butter pud with prunes and dried apricots, and chocolate bread and butter pudding now has a fourth contender in the best-of-the-best stakes. Here it is. You may make it with croissants or with bread if you prefer. It is the rhubarb and ginger that give the heart-stopping creamy, eggy butteriness a shock of sharpness – cutting the richness with fruit and spice perfectly.

My 12-year-old friend Izzy, a keen cook who lives in the village, helped me make this when I dreamt it up and I promised, in return, that she would get a mention if the pudding were good enough for this book.

serves 8

for the fruit layer

1kg/2¼lb rhubarb, trimmed and cut into short lengths

180g/6oz demerara or unrefined granulated sugar

finely grated zest and juice of 1 orange

1 ball stem ginger preserved in syrup, finely diced, plus 3 tbsp syrup from the jar

for the custard layer

300ml/½ pint Jersey or full-cream milk

300ml/½ pint Jersey or double cream

1 vanilla pod, split, seeds scraped out

3 organic large eggs

120g/4½oz vanilla caster sugar

for the bread layer

4 high-quality brioches or all-butter croissants

Preheat the oven to 180°C/Gas 4. Put the rhubarb into a wide, shallow, heavy-bottomed pan. Scatter over the sugar, orange zest and juice, and the ginger with its syrup. Place over a medium heat and move the rhubarb around carefully, so as not to break it up. Cook until the sugar has dissolved and the fruit is at the stage where it is a little mulchy but still retaining its shape. Remove the rhubarb to a sieve and allow the juice to drip into a bowl beneath; save the juice for the glaze.

For the custard, pour the milk and cream into a heavy-bottomed pan and add the vanilla seeds and pod. Heat slowly, removing the pan from the heat before the liquid boils. Meanwhile, whisk the eggs and sugar together in a bowl. Strain the infused milk and pour onto the egg mixture, whisking well.

Split the brioches or croissants in half horizontally. Place the bottom halves in a single layer in a greased baking dish and plop the rhubarb evenly over the surface. Arrange the brioche or croissant top halves over the rhubarb and pour the custard mixture evenly over the top.

Stand the baking dish in a large roasting tin and pour in enough boiling water to come halfway up the sides of the baking dish. Bake in the middle of the oven for 40–50 minutes until the custard is set through. A faint wobble in the middle is fine as the dish will continue cooking as it cools.

Leave the pudding in the bain-marie to keep it warm. Meanwhile, for the glaze, pour the reserved rhubarb syrup into a small pan and bubble over a medium heat to reduce by half until thick and jammy. Brush over the top of the pudding to give a luscious pink glaze. Serve hot or warm, with pouring cream.

Baked peach brown Betty

I love the lightness of a Betty when a crumble seems too heavy – in this case a lovely roasted peach with the crunch of buttery crumb and amaretti. The end result is definitely a whole fruit, not a purée or a compote. You can also make it using nectarines, plums, greengages or apricots. If you do not have any amaretti or similar Italian biscuits, use extra crumbs and add a little natural almond extract with the sugar.

serves 6

6 medium or 3 large ripe peaches, ideally white

90g/3oz brown breadcrumbs

juice of ½ lemon (if peeling the peaches)

4 tbsp light muscovado sugar

1 glass pudding wine, Pedro Ximénez or oloroso sherry

6 amaretti biscuits

60g/2oz unsalted butter

Preheat the oven to 180°C/Gas 4. Choose a gratin dish or heavy-bottomed ovenproof pan that will hold the peaches, once halved, snugly. Scatter the breadcrumbs on a baking tray and toast in the oven for 5 minutes or until dry.

If you prefer to skin the peaches, steep them in a bowl of boiling hot water for a minute, then remove and peel away the skins. Halve and stone the fruit and rub the cut surfaces with a little lemon juice. Put the peach halves cut-side up in the baking dish and sprinkle with 1 tbsp of the muscovado sugar. Pour the wine or sherry around them.

Crush the amaretti into the toasted breadcrumbs, add the remaining sugar and mix well. Sprinkle a layer of the crumb mixture over the peach halves and dot with butter. Bake for 30 minutes or until the peaches are cooked and the topping is bubbling and brown.

Serve with plenty of whipped cream, into which you might like to whisk 1–2 tbsp pêche de vigne if you have some.

Pain perdu with fruit compote

In medieval times this lovely, simple dish was eaten in both England and France. It was originally made from bread baked with the finest flour, which was dipped in beaten egg before frying, spicing and sugaring. It really is as good for breakfast or brunch as it is for pudding.

For the compote, I love to combine strawberries and rhubarb when strawberries are in season. A mix of blueberries, strawberries and raspberries is also delicious: toss in half the amount of sugar suggested for the rhubarb and briefly warm in a pan – just to get the juices flowing.

serves 4

4 slices good day-old bread, crusts removed if preferred

4 tbsp single cream

3 organic large eggs

1 tbsp sherry or Madeira

large knob of unsalted butter

1–2 tsp vanilla caster sugar

½ tsp ground cinnamon, ideally freshly ground

for the compote

500g/1lb 2oz rhubarb, cut into short lengths on the diagonal

4 tbsp light muscovado or unrefined granulated sugar

250g/9oz strawberries (Gariguette if you can find them, not the ubiquitous, acidic Elsanta), halved

Cut each slice of bread into two triangles. Whisk the cream, eggs and sherry or Madeira together in a bowl.

Now start the compote: put the rhubarb into a heavy-bottomed frying pan and scatter over the sugar. Cook over a moderate heat until just tender but still holding its shape, turning carefully from time to time so as not to break up the fruit.

Meanwhile, melt a good knob of butter in a frying pan until foaming but not brown. Dunk each slice of bread in the creamy mixture, turning to soak both sides. Slip the triangles of dunked bread into the pan and fry on both sides until golden brown and crisp.

When the rhubarb is almost ready, toss in the strawberries and heat through for a couple of minutes.

Lay the pain perdu in a warmed serving dish and sprinkle lightly with a little caster sugar mixed with cinnamon. Serve with the fruit compote.

Summer pudding

To my mind, nothing speaks more obviously of summer, abundance and sheer fruitiness than a summer pudding. Here I am not reinventing the wheel, I'm just using less bread and defining the fruits more clearly by cooking them separately. Raspberries and blackberries are classic partners, though strawberries can be part of the equation too. Cherries and redcurrants in their short seasons are lovely additions, while blueberries can stand in at other times. I tend to avoid blackcurrants, as they are inclined to dominate. Of course, you can make individual puddings if you prefer. Do remember the pudding needs to be made a day ahead and refrigerated overnight.

serves 6–8

a day-old loaf of good white bread, sliced and crusts removed

450g/1lb raspberries

about 120g/4oz vanilla caster sugar

300g/10oz strawberries, sliced

1 tbsp kirsch

200g/7oz blackberries

2 tbsp crème de cassis

200g/7oz blueberries, or use redcurrants or stoned cherries in season

spritz of lemon juice

unrefined icing sugar to taste

Preheat the oven to 150°C/Gas 2. Lay the bread slices on a large baking sheet and place in the oven for 5–10 minutes to dry out.

Set aside a third of the raspberries for the sauce. Throw the rest into a wide, heavy-bottomed pan, sprinkle with 1 tbsp sugar and heat gently until the fruit just starts to bleed but does not lose its shape. Instantly tip into a bowl. Repeat with all of the strawberries, adding 1 tbsp kirsch and scattering a scant tbsp of sugar over them. Next the blackberries, with 1 tbsp cassis and a heaped tbsp of sugar and finally the blueberries with 1 tbsp sugar and 1 tbsp cassis again, to bring out their flavour.

Cut a circle of bread to fit the bottom of a 1.2 litre/2 pint pudding basin and press into position. Spoon a layer of fruit and juice on top. Add another bread round and a different layer of fruit, then repeat two or three times to fill the basin. You need room for a final layer of bread.

Put a saucer or plate on top of the pudding that just fits inside the basin and place some heavy weights on top. Refrigerate overnight.

The next day, for the sauce, blitz the reserved raspberries in a blender or food processor, then sieve and add a spritz of lemon and icing sugar to taste. Turn the pudding out onto a serving plate and pour the raspberry sauce over. Serve with lashings of clotted cream.

Supper for a song

I feel I have sung for my supper all my life, although I was pretty scratchy and out of tune when I started, in fact I simply didn't have a clue.

It all began at university where the food was really so bad that I decided to teach myself to cook. I had to invent supper for a song every night and in the absence of money I had to make do. To begin with, I didn't know whether I had even a modicum of talent for cooking and whatever I might have was, as yet, unharnessed to any skills or knowledge. But I had greed, an appetite for good food and an appetite to learn how to cook, which remain undimmed. I didn't see the desire to cook a good dinner as an inferior pastime like some of my fellow students. I guess I didn't realise back then that I was setting out on a way of life where good food would always play a vital role.

I started cooking every night and slowly the triumphs began to overtake the disasters, and my growing confidence and technique turned budding love to burning obsession. Food is my passion – well, one of them – and continues to be 30 years since I cooked my first dinner. Cooking became part of the fabric of my life, and then my life: I could never not sing for my supper. I still take the greatest pride in inventing suppers for a song, the most creative and satisfying way of cooking.

And always with a song. Music and cooking are mighty fine accompaniments. I simply have no idea how Saturday afternoons would pass without cooking to 'Jazz Record Request', any more than the evenings would begin in earnest without the dulcet tones of Sean Rafferty's 'In Tune' on Radio 3. When my son Harry is at home I have my very own resident minstrel plus guitar, for which I'm happy to offer the ultimate reward, supper for a song.

Cooking a good supper is the best way to win friends and influence and disarm enemies. Getting people to talk round a kitchen table is one thing; give them food and friendship follows. Well, that's what I've found ever since my fledgling attempts at nineteen in an ill-equipped kitchen with the most basic ingredients, a few simple recipes and a group of starving students.

If the purse strings are tight but you have passion, imagination and a dedication to the table, you can cook a good dinner. And cooking for friends around you, whatever your budget – you can always ask them to contribute – is part of the same idea, part of the great communal feast of life, which isn't about extravagance and showing off, it's about good food and good company.

Here are some of my favourite dishes and dinners. Sometimes the luxury of something special like fine wild salmon might not appear, at first glance, to be part of the supper-for-a-song hymn sheet, but look a little closer, see how all the surrounding ingredients and accompanying dishes are chosen to minimise the one extravagance, something we can all do with a little thought.

Have a bit of a splurge one day, cook a something-out-of-nothing supper (see pages 164–185) the next. Don't make false or misery-inducing economies. Great taste foremost, uppermost, not just most, but all of the time.

Let the gastronomic aria commence.

Crushed peas with feta and spring onions

This is a lovely dish to serve with griddled pita bread, either alongside a couple of other mezze while you have a drink before supper, or as a starter in its own right, or as a light lunch with a good salad on the side. In the summer please use fresh peas, at all other times of year the wondrous frozen pea will do. You can make this dish in advance, put it in the fridge and bring it back to room temperature when you want it.

serves 4–6 as a starter

1kg/2¼lb peas in the pod, or 250g/9oz frozen organic peas or petit pois

2–4 tbsp fruity olive oil

200g/7oz packet sheep's milk feta, drained

200g/7oz Greek yoghurt

1 garlic clove, peeled and finely chopped with a little sea salt

a bunch of spring onions, trimmed and finely sliced

a large handful of mint leaves, shredded

juice of 1 lemon

sea salt and black pepper

If using fresh peas, shell them and cook briefly in boiling water until al dente, then drain well and tip into a large bowl. Sprinkle with 2 tbsp olive oil and crush them coarsely with a potato masher.

If you are using frozen peas, blanch them briefly, drain exceptionally well and crush before adding the oil, pouring off any more excess water at this stage; add the oil bit by bit and less liberally.

Mash the feta and yoghurt together in a shallow bowl. While the peas are still hot, tip in the feta and toss to combine. This is all about texture, not smooth dippiness. Add the chopped garlic.

Now add the spring onions and 2 tbsp shredded mint. Stir in the juice of ½ lemon to start with. Season with pepper and a little salt if you think it is needed, feta is pretty salty. Taste and adjust the seasoning, adding more lemon juice, mint or olive oil if you like.

Serve in a shallow dish with a mound of warm, griddled pita bread.

Pea, mint and scallop custards

Years ago the brilliant chef Rowley Leigh, now at Le Café Anglais, then at Kensington Place, came up with a delectable dish of scallops served on a minted pea purée. It was one of those elegantly simple, understated things that owed everything to the understanding of restraint, of not going a flavour too far.

But it is another dish I have been cooking for years, a crab custard, that led me to wonder about making a creamy, crushed pea and mint custard, concealing scallops and their hectically coloured coral beneath, until you hit the last mouthful. It worked a treat. Adding the white of the scallop whole and raw, the coral likewise, means they poach perfectly without overcooking. Two small scallops or one large one per ramekin is hardly the price of a mortgage. This dish is one I will make and make.

serves 6 as a starter

12 medium or 6 large scallops, cleaned

45g/1½oz unsalted butter

4 heaped tbsp Jersey or double cream

250g/9oz frozen organic petit pois

2 organic large eggs, beaten, plus 3 extra yolks

8–10 mint leaves, finely chopped

sea salt and black pepper

Preheat the oven to 180°C/Gas 4. Separate the corals from the scallop discs, keeping them whole; set both aside.

Melt the butter in a pan, add 3 heaped tbsp of the cream and heat to scalding point. Now add the peas and stir them until they are just cooked through, about 5 minutes.

Remove from the heat and add the last of the cream. Beat in the egg yolks, one by one, followed by the beaten eggs. Stir in about three-quarters of the mint and some seasoning.

Scrape the mixture into a blender and blitz so briefly that you can barely count to 3. The whole point is to keep the peas rough-textured, not smooth. Taste again, and if you need to, add the last of the mint, which should scent but not intrude.

Boil a kettle. Meanwhile, plop one or two white scallops and their corals into the bottom of each of 6 ramekins. Spoon the pea mixture over the top. Stand the ramekins in a roasting tin and pour in enough boiling water to come halfway up their sides. Lay an oiled piece of greaseproof paper over the top to stop a skin forming on the custards.

Cook in the centre of the oven for 20 minutes. Give the roasting tin a little shake to check the custards. They should have set; if not give them another 5 minutes.

Remove the ramekins from the roasting tin and place each one on a small plate. Serve warm.

Spiced chicken liver mousse with blackened onions

This dish is inspired by my favourite starter at The Malabar, an Indian restaurant in Notting Hill – fried whole chicken livers coated in blackened onions, which arrives on a sizzling karahi. The soft meat with the spiced, crunchy onion is divine.

These little spicy ramekins of liver are as smooth as silk with a hint of fennel seed, coriander and cumin. I serve them with griddled spice-coated onions and fingers of toast. The mousse is rich, so a small ramekin is really enough. Serve warm or cold.

serves 6–8 as a starter

400g/14oz organic chicken livers, trimmed of all sinew

a little milk to soak

1½ tsp fennel seeds

1 tsp cumin seeds

1 tsp coriander seeds

½ tsp cayenne pepper

2 organic large eggs, plus 3 extra yolks

250ml/8½fl oz double cream

150ml/¼ pint milk

50g/2oz butter, melted and cooled to tepid

sea salt and black pepper

for the blackened onions

1 large onion, peeled and sliced

a little olive oil to coat

½ tsp dried chilli flakes

1½ tsp nigella (black onion) seeds

1 tsp ground turmeric

1½ tsp toasted cumin seeds

to serve

a small handful of coriander leaves, chopped (optional)

toast fingers

Put the chicken livers into a bowl, pour on enough milk to cover and leave to soak for an hour or so. Preheat the oven to 150°C/Gas 2. Lightly grease 6–8 small ramekins with butter.

Pour off the milk from the chicken livers and dry them on kitchen paper. Toast the fennel and cumin seeds gently for about a minute in a dry pan until they start to release their fragrance; don't let them over-brown. Tip into a mortar and crush together with the coriander seeds.

Put the chicken livers into a blender and add the crushed spices, cayenne, eggs and extra yolks, cream, milk and melted butter. Season. Blend for about 5 minutes – longer than seems sane. Push the mixture through a sieve with a wooden spoon into a bowl.

Boil a kettle. Divide the mixture between the ramekins. Stand them in a roasting tin and pour in enough boiling water to come halfway up their sides. Lay a sheet of greased greaseproof paper on top and cook in the middle of the oven for 35 minutes.

Meanwhile, for the blackened onions, toss the sliced onion in a bowl with a little olive oil, then add the spices and some seasoning and turn to coat. Heat a griddle, or a heavy-bottomed pan if you don't have one. When it is really hot, throw on the onion slices and cook until they have browned and charred in places. They will not soften quite enough on the griddle, so transfer them to a heated frying pan to finish cooking, adding a little more oil if they begin to stick. Taste and adjust the spicing and seasoning.

When the mousses are cooked, remove from the oven and leave to stand in the bain-marie for 10 minutes.

To turn out, run a small, sharp knife around the edge of each mousse and invert onto a plate. Put a little heap of blackened onions next to each one and scatter over a little chopped coriander if you like. Serve with hot toast.

Pickled mackerel and potato salad

This refreshing, vibrant dish is great to start a supper with. Get pickling the night before you want to eat it, and get your fishmonger to skin and fillet the mackerel, which must be spanking fresh.

serves 6 as a starter

3 mackerel, skinned and filleted, pin bones removed

for the marinade

125ml/4fl oz olive oil

125ml/4fl oz dry white wine

50ml/2fl oz white wine vinegar

2 tbsp Pernod

1 organic lemon, thinly sliced

2 bay leaves

2 sprigs each of parsley, dill and thyme

1 carrot, finely sliced

1 celery stalk, de-strung with a potato peeler and finely sliced

1 shallot or small red onion, peeled and finely sliced

1 level tbsp muscovado sugar

pinch of sea salt

6 white peppercorns

chopped dill or chives to serve (optional)

for the potato salad

450g/1lb waxy salad potatoes, like Jersey, Anya, Pink Fir Apple

1 shallot, peeled and finely chopped

4 tbsp olive oil, or more

1 tbsp white wine or tarragon vinegar

2 tbsp chopped flat-leaf parsley

sea salt and black pepper

Check the mackerel fillets for any pin bones, then cut into strips, about 4cm/1½ inches long and 1cm/½ inch wide. Mix all the marinade ingredients together in a sealable glass or plastic container and add the mackerel strips. Make sure they are submerged in the marinade, seal the container and refrigerate for 12–18 hours.

A couple of hours before you want to eat it, make the salad. Boil the potatoes until just tender, then drain and slice them while hot. Toss into a bowl and mix with all the other salad ingredients. Check the seasoning and set aside until ready to serve. You may need to add a little more olive oil later as the potatoes absorb a lot, and you may need to sharpen them up with a little more vinegar.

When ready to serve, place a generous spoonful of potato salad on each plate and top with strips of marinated mackerel and the marinade vegetables. You may wish to sprinkle over a little chopped dill or chives.

Carrot, apple and blue cheese soup

I think I must have been thinking ploughman's lunch in a bowl for this, but the combination of sweet carrot, sharp apple and salty cheese works brilliantly.

When I am making soups, I regularly use water if I haven't any stock to hand and look for something else to create body. More often than not I will find a strong, vibrant ingredient to do this, lending depth and clarity. The three main ingredients in this soup all play a role in defining its character.

serves 4 as a starter

2–3 tbsp olive oil

1 small red or white onion, peeled and finely chopped

1 garlic clove, peeled and finely chopped

sea salt and black pepper

1 giant organic carrot, finely diced

1 large cooking apple

1.2 litres/2 pints water

60–90g/2–3oz good blue cheese like Beenleigh, Stilton, Stichelton

Warm the olive oil in a large, heavy-bottomed pan and sauté the onion and garlic with a sprinkle of salt to help the onion juices run, over a medium heat for a few minutes. Add the carrot, stir to coat in the oil and cook for about 10 minutes until it is beginning to soften.

Meanwhile, peel, quarter and core the apple and cut into slices. Add to the pan and cook together for a couple of minutes.

Add the water, a ladleful at a time so that it heats up more quickly. Bring to a simmer, put the lid on and continue to simmer for 10 minutes. Remove from the heat and season with pepper only.

Liquidise the soup in a blender in batches as necessary, crumbling in the blue cheese as you do so. Taste critically. You may need a little more cheese, you may need to adjust the seasoning.

Return the soup to the pan and bring to a simmer again before serving.

Middle Eastern stuffed peppers

I don't quite know how stuffed peppers got a bad name and became something of a joke. It must have been down to horribly stuffed, semi-raw peppers, filled with dried-up rice and greasy mince. In reality, a well-stuffed pepper is a beauty to behold and to eat – and just as good cold the next day. This is how I cooked mine in Ireland this summer and I'm still not sure whether hot, warm or cold takes pole position – they were all lovely.

If there are two of you, keep 4 stuffed pepper halves for another meal. Cool, then refrigerate, bringing them up to room temperature an hour before you want to eat them cold. They will need a little more olive oil sprinkled over them the following day and perhaps some freshly chopped parsley and/or mint and a little more toasted cumin.

serves 4

4 peppers, red and yellow, or all red

for the stuffing

225g/8oz brown basmati rice

½ cinnamon stick

4 cardamom pods

about 5 tbsp olive oil

1 medium onion, peeled and finely chopped

1 carrot, peeled and diced

2 garlic cloves, peeled and sliced

1 courgette, cut into small dice

½ tsp cayenne pepper, or to taste

1 tsp ground ginger

2–3 tbsp leftover tomato sauce of any kind (see page 174), or tinned organic cherry tomatoes in juice

2 tbsp pine nuts, toasted in the oven or a dry pan

a handful of raisins, soaked in warm water for 30 minutes

a small bunch of coriander, leaves stripped and chopped

sea salt and black pepper

3–4 ladlefuls chicken stock

chopped parsley or mint, to finish (optional)

Preheat the oven to 200°C/Gas 6. Cut the peppers in half vertically through their stalks and remove their seeds and white membranes. Place cut side up in a baking dish.

Cook the rice, according to the instructions on the packet, with the cinnamon and cardamom, until al dente.

Meanwhile, heat 2 tbsp olive oil in a large, heavy-bottomed frying pan, then add the chopped onion and carrot, turning them to coat. Cook over a medium heat for about 5 minutes, then add the garlic and courgette, with the cayenne and ginger. Keep stirring for a few minutes until everything is turning translucent and softening.

Add your leftover tomato sauce or tinned tomatoes in juice at this point, stirring them in. Cook for another 5 minutes or so, then take off the heat and add the toasted pine nuts, drained raisins, chopped coriander and seasoning.

When the rice is ready, drain it well and discard the spices. Add enough of the cooked rice to the vegetable mixture to ensure a well-balanced stuffing that doesn't err on the side of too much basmati. (You can keep any leftover rice to dress up as a spiced rice salad and eat cold.) Add a little of the chicken stock to the mixture to lubricate the rice; again, use your judgement.

Spoon the mixture into the pepper halves in the baking dish, piling it up generously. Add a few ladlefuls of stock to the dish and dribble some olive oil over each pepper half.

Cover the top of the roasting tin with a sheet of oiled greaseproof paper to prevent the rice drying out. Bake for 40–45 minutes, checking the peppers after 20 minutes or so, as you may need to add a little more stock to the roasting tin.

Serve the peppers hot, warm or cold, scattered with chopped parsley or mint if you like.

Stuffed squid

The stuffing for the Middle Eastern peppers on the previous page is every bit as good in squid pouches, gently poached in red wine. The thing about squid is there's no middle way. Cook it short and hot or cook it long and slow and you have meaty tenderness. Anything else and you may as well chew a blanket. Red wine and black ink, the little frilly bits and the stuffed, giant pockets submerged beneath the vino and you have a lovely dish to serve with an extra green vegetable on the side. And at a couple of quid a pocket, this is fish for our financial times.

serves 2

2 medium squid, about 250g/9oz each

about ⅓ quantity rice stuffing (from Middle Eastern peppers, page 133)

a handful of peas and/or skinned broad beans

sea salt and black pepper

about 350ml/12fl oz red wine

a little good olive oil (optional)

a handful of flat-leaf parsley, chopped (optional)

Preheat the oven to 150°C/Gas 2. Clean the squid by pulling the tentacles and head from the body. Cut off the tentacles and discard the head. Remove the transparent quill from the body pouch and the soft, gooey bits. Keep the ink sacs (or you can buy a sachet of squid ink from the fishmonger if your squid is ready prepared). Rinse the body pouches and tentacles.

Have the stuffing ready. Stir the broad beans and/or peas into the mixture and check the seasoning. Stuff the squid pouches three-quarters full with the mixture, no more or they will burst. Lay them next to each other snugly in a baking dish and add the tentacles.

Heat the red wine in a pan, then pour enough into the baking dish to come halfway up the sides of the stuffed squid. Add the squid ink. Cover the dish with foil and braise in the oven for 2½ hours, turning the squid over halfway through the cooking time. Insert a skewer into the squid to check that it is tender; it may need another 30 minutes. The white squid flesh colours a lovely rusty garnet in the inky wine.

Leave to stand for 10 minutes out of the oven. You may like to add a libation of olive oil and a scattering of parsley before serving.

Wild salmon
with smoked aubergine polenta and hot cucumber

It is not just that I am driven by the seasons, it is that I could not contemplate eating farmed salmon. Beg to differ if you will, but I would rather one fine Irish salmon from the Bundorragha or the Bunowen rivers in Co. Mayo in the summer than eat farmed salmon steaks through the year. Wild Alaskan salmon doesn't have quite the flavour of my Atlantic heroes, but it is in such a different league to the farmed that I can only urge you to experiment.

Here the quality of real polenta with the subterfuge, smoky surprise of the aubergine and the pale green still-crisp cucumber, both a steal, offset any perceived extravagance. Seek out proper polenta. Made with yellow maize flour, it is the colour of egg yolk and far superior to quick-cook polenta, which has no discernible flavour.

The colours are exquisite in this dish, though quite how I came upon the unusual combination I cannot recall. It is pure heaven, I assure you, and needs no extras.

serves 4

4 wild salmon fillets
knob of unsalted butter
sea salt and black pepper

for the polenta

400–500g/14oz–1lb 2oz
coarse-grain yellow polenta,
depending on appetite (I use
Il Saraceno)

2 litres/3½ pints water

2–3 tsp salt

1 aubergine

large knob of butter

for the cucumber

1 cucumber

small knob of unsalted butter

about 150ml/¼ pint double
cream

2 heaped tsp chopped
tarragon

For the polenta, bring the water to the boil in a large, wide, heavy-bottomed pan. Add 2–3 tsp salt. Pour in the polenta slowly, in a steady stream, stirring with a whisk until smooth. At this stage, over a high heat, the mixture will splutter and jump out of the pan, so wrap a cloth around your hand and stir with a long-handled wooden spoon. After 5 minutes you may turn the heat down and stir less regularly over the next 40–50 minutes.

In the meantime, prick the aubergine in a few places with the tip of a knife. Hold it with a pair of tongs over a charcoal grill or gas flame and char it thoroughly on all sides. It should cook through in 5 minutes or so, but test with a skewer. Alternatively you can roast the aubergine in the oven at 190°C/Gas 5 until tender, although you will not attain the smokiness.

Remove the cooked aubergine to a bowl, cover with cling film and leave until you can handle it, then peel away all the charred skin. Put the luscious flesh into a bowl and mash it coarsely with a fork.

Peel the cucumber and halve it lengthways, then scoop the seeds out with a small teaspoon. Cut into short lengths.

About 5 minutes before the polenta is likely to be ready, you should start to cook the fish and cucumber.

Melt a little knob of butter in a pan and add the cucumber with a pinch of salt. Cook for a couple of minutes, then add the cream and tarragon and continue to cook until the sauce thickens and the cucumber is still crisp, yet not resistant. Check the seasoning and remove from the heat.

At the same time, heat a knob of butter in a heavy-bottomed frying pan. Season the salmon fillets and place them skin side down in the bubbling butter. Cook over a medium heat until you can see that the flesh has turned a pale pink colour halfway up the thickness. Turn over and repeat but leave a slim stripe of flamingo-bright flesh when you remove the salmon – overcooking fish happens in a whisker.

Keep an eye on the polenta while you cook the fish and cucumber. It will come away from the sides of the pan when it is cooked. At this point, remove it from the heat, add a large knob of butter, season and stir in the mashed aubergine.

Slop a goodly portion of polenta onto each warmed plate. Perch the salmon on the top and serve a spoonful of cucumber in tarragon cream on the side.

Little John Dory fillets
with braised fennel and anchovy butter

In the winter months, my fishmonger Chris tells me, baby John Dory is a steal. So I buy it and try it immediately. You need three small fillets per person and they need little more than a brief introduction to the pan. Braised fennel and a simple anchovy butter are ideal accompaniments. A glimmer of green parsley stops this from being an all-white with a-hint-of-pink dish. In the summer months when the fish are bigger, adjust their cooking time accordingly.

serves 2

6 John Dory fillets, about 200–225g/7–8oz fish per person

1 large fennel bulb

a little lemon juice

2 tbsp olive oil

1 tsp finely chopped rosemary needles

small glass white wine

sea salt and black pepper

knob of unsalted butter

1 tsp very finely chopped flat-leaf parsley

for the anchovy butter

60g/2oz butter, softened to room temperature

3 good-quality anchovies

a little lemon juice

First make the anchovy butter. Put two-thirds of the butter on a small plate and mash in the anchovies until you have a marbled, rather than a uniform pink effect. Add a little spritz of lemon juice and a hint of salt and pepper, then put the butter on a butter paper or piece of greaseproof paper and roll it into a cylindrical shape, close the paper around it and freeze for 30 minutes or longer. That way you can cut it from frozen and drop it onto the fish when it's cooked.

Have the fish fillets ready at room temperature. Remove any tough outer leaves from the fennel, then slice the bulb as finely as you possibly can, using a mandolin. Immediately spritz a little lemon juice over the fennel slices to stop discoloration.

Heat 1 tbsp olive oil in a frying pan and when hot, add the chopped rosemary. Wait 30 seconds until it fizzles, then add the fennel and stir to coat. Lower the heat so that the fennel cooks down slowly. After a few minutes pour in the wine and let it bubble and begin to reduce. Season. Cook until you have a softened tangle, then transfer to a warm plate with the juice; keep warm.

Add the knob of butter to the pan and heat. When it begins to foam, lay the fish fillets in the pan skin side down and season them. Fry over a medium heat for a couple of minutes or until the flesh is translucent halfway up the fillets. Flip them over carefully so that they don't break up and the delicate skin doesn't tear. Cook until opaque, another minute or two, then take off the heat.

Spoon the fennel onto warmed plates and lay the fillets on top. Slice the chilled anchovy butter into rounds and place one on top of each fillet. Scatter the parsley over and serve. Green and orange veg on the side – to add further colour and texture – and some mash, work well.

Braised chicken and rice
with orange, saffron, almond and pistachio syrup

Here is a jewel of an Afghani dish. Unusual and exotic, it is one I cook regularly, sometimes with shoulder of lamb instead of chicken thighs. I serve it with slow-cooked spinach, finished with leeks and a minuscule amount of rhubarb. This may sound strange but the rhubarb is sweetened by the leeks and it really does work.

If Seville oranges are not in season and you are cooking this dish in the summer with sweeter orange peel, just halve the quantity of sugar.

serves 4

450g/1lb brown basmati rice

4 tbsp olive oil

2 medium onions, peeled and finely chopped

sea salt and black pepper

4 large chicken thighs, chopped in half, or 8 smaller ones

570ml/1 pint water, plus 110ml/3½fl oz for the syrup

1 large organic Seville or other orange

25g/1oz unrefined granulated sugar

50g/2oz flaked blanched almonds

50g/2oz shelled pistachio nuts, chopped

large pinch of saffron stamens

25ml/1fl oz rosewater

7–8 cardamom pods, lightly crushed, seeds extracted

a handful of blanched, skinned baby broad beans (optional)

a handful of blanched peas (optional)

Rinse the rice in a sieve under cold running water until the water runs clear; put to one side.

Heat the olive oil in a large, heavy-bottomed pot and throw in the onions. Cook over a medium heat until they soften and turn golden. Season the chicken thighs and add them to the pan. Brown on all sides, then pour in 570ml/1 pint water and bring to a simmer. Cover with a lid and cook until the chicken is tender, about 20 minutes.

Meanwhile, peel the zest from the orange with a potato peeler, then cut it into matchstick strips. Blanch in a small pan of boiling water for a couple of minutes, then drain.

Dissolve the sugar in 110ml/3½fl oz water in a small, heavy-bottomed pan over a medium heat, then bring to the boil and let bubble to reduce and thicken for 5–10 minutes until syrupy. Add the orange zest, flaked almonds and pistachios and boil for 5 minutes, skimming off any froth. Strain the syrup and return to the pan; set aside the orange zest and nuts. Add the saffron and rosewater to the syrup and boil again for 3 minutes, then add the cardamom seeds.

Preheat the oven to 150°C/Gas 2. Strain the stock from the chicken thighs and add the syrup to it. Make this up to 570ml/1 pint with more water. Bring it to the boil in an ovenproof pan and add the rice. Season and add two-thirds of the orange zest and nuts, keeping the rest to one side. Bring back to the boil, then cover and simmer until the rice is cooked. The liquid should have all been absorbed by now.

Bury the chicken and onions in the rice and add the broad beans and peas if you are including them. Put the lid on and cook in the oven for 20 minutes.

Serve straight from the pan or, if you prefer, in a large, warmed serving dish. Sprinkle the last third of the orange zest and nuts over the top before bringing it to the table.

Stuffed pork fillet with figs and Marsala

This is a simple but beauteous marriage, or rather a double marriage. The four main ingredients – pork, figs, black pudding and Marsala – partner and complement each other, without any one of them overwhelming the other. It only takes minutes to flatten, stuff, tie and brown the pork, the black pudding deepening the flavour of the meat and stretching it.

When you cut the pork and see the black pud encased in white meat – juicy, tender and sticky with sweet Marsala and figs – you know you have a dish worthy of a dinner party or a special, but simple-to-prepare supper.

Please make this with properly reared pork. The fast-bred industrially reared pigs taste how you would expect after such an unpleasant life. The old breeds who have been cavorting and truffling in the mud and had time to lay down a proper coating of fat and flavoursome meat are altogether different.

serves 4

1 organic, free-range pork fillet

a few sprigs of thyme, leaves stripped and chopped

sea salt and black pepper

1 small or ½ large black pudding

1 tbsp olive oil

45g/1½oz butter, or so

2–3 glasses Marsala, sweet not dry

4 fresh figs, halved

Preheat the oven to 180°C/Gas 4. Slice down through the middle of the pork fillet with a sharp knife to the point at which you can open it out like a book, but it remains in one piece. Sprinkle with a little of the thyme and some sea salt. Take the pudding out of its jacket and crumble it along the middle of the pork fillet, not quite to the ends. Roll up the pork and tie it at intervals with string.

Heat the olive oil and a knob of butter in a frying pan, large enough to take the pork fillet, until it is foaming. Add the meat and brown on all sides for a few minutes, then remove to a plate and season with salt and pepper.

Pour off any fat that looks brown, then deglaze the pan with a glass of Marsala, letting it bubble and reduce by about half. Pour in another glass and reduce a little more, then sprinkle in 1 tsp chopped thyme. Stir in a knob of butter, cut into small pieces, to make the sauce glossy. Add the halved figs and warm for 30 seconds.

Lay the pork fillet in the centre of a sheet of greaseproof paper, large enough to enclose it in a baggy parcel. Plop some figs on top and place the rest alongside. Pour the Marsala sauce over the top. Close the parcel by folding up the sides and ends securely and fastening with paper clips. Place on a baking tray and cook in the oven for 25 minutes.

Let the meat rest en papillote for 5 minutes before unwrapping and lifting onto a board. Carve into thick slices and arrange with the figs on a warmed platter or on individual plates. Tip the sauce into a pan and reheat until bubbling, then pour it over the meat. Add a last sprinkle of thyme and serve, with mash and something green.

Liver and onions
with chilli, lime and fish sauce

Yes, fish sauce. Nothing so odd in Asian or Chinese cooking about marrying shrimp paste or fish sauce with beef or pork and we traditionally spike anchovy into roast lamb to deepen and underscore the flavour without the effect being at all fishy. That is what this dish is about.

You may make it with lamb's or calf's liver, but the less expensive pig's liver is quite a difficult one to convince people of, and I'm trying to do that here. The pigginess can be overpowering, but not in this case – it's the best dish of liver I've eaten in a long time. The liver came from an organic Middle White pig. Buying a pig by the half or the quarter, with a neighbour or two, is a cost effective way of getting a properly-reared traditional-breed beast of the highest quality.

serves 2

450g/1lb or so pig's liver, in 2 thick tranches

2–3 tbsp fino sherry

1 tbsp red wine vinegar

2 large onions, peeled (I used one red, one white)

3 tbsp olive oil

sea salt and black pepper

1 tsp sugar

1 kashmiri hot dried chilli, crushed, or 1 tsp dried chilli flakes

1 heaped tbsp plain flour

1 tbsp Thai fish sauce

juice of 1 lime

a slug of red wine (whatever you happen to be drinking)

Put the liver into a shallow dish, pour on the sherry and wine vinegar and leave to marinate in a cool place for a couple of hours, turning it over several times.

Meanwhile, slice the onions as finely as you possibly can. Heat 1 tbsp olive oil in a heavy-bottomed pan, add the onions with a little salt and sweat gently until they wilt. Sprinkle with the sugar and black pepper, cover with the lid and continue to cook gently, stirring from time to time, for a further 20 minutes or so. Remove from the heat.

Drain the liver and dry on both sides with kitchen paper. Mix the crushed chilli and some seasoning with the flour on a plate. Heat 2 tbsp olive oil in a large, heavy-bottomed frying pan over a brisk heat.

Dip the liver in the chilli flour, coating both sides and shaking any excess off, then add to the sizzling oil. Brown for a good 3 minutes if the slices are thick. You will see the cooking process happen, the brown creeping up the red liver as it fries. When it reaches halfway up each slice, flip the liver over and continue to cook for 30 seconds or so.

Add the fish sauce and let it almost bubble away, then pour in the lime juice, followed by the wine. The moment the liver is cooked, remove it to a warm plate; it should still be pink in the middle.

Scrape and deglaze the pan, throw in the cooked onions and reheat for a minute. Tip them and the juices over the liver and serve with roasted roots and a good helping of mashed potato.

Roasted roots

Preheat oven to 200°C/Gas 6. Peel and slice 1 parsnip and 1 carrot into long, chunky fingers, parboil for 2–3 minutes and drain well. Toss together in a bowl with 1 diced, peeled medium beetroot, 1 tbsp olive oil, 1 tbsp runny honey and 1 tbsp sesame seeds. Heat another 1 tbsp olive oil in a small roasting tray in the oven. After a few minutes, slosh the vegetables into the hot oil and roast for 25–30 minutes until cooked and gooey, turning to brown them all over. Season to taste and serve.

Prune clafoutis

The original clafoutis from Limousin was made with the region's cherries, but the dish is just as gorgeous in the summer made with raspberries and figs, apricots, greengages or plums.

Midwinter is all about batter pudding, which essentially this is, so I thought I would try making a wintry clafoutis with luscious Agen prunes steeped in an orange liqueur. The final touch to take this out of the realms of sweet Yorkshire pud was to gratinée it. Serve it with some crème fraîche with a little orange zest and Cointreau whisked in and it really is heaven.

serves 6

for the prunes

400g/14oz stoned Agen prunes

1 heaped tbsp vanilla sugar

2 tbsp Cointreau

butter and sugar for the baking dish, plus a little cinnamon (optional)

for the batter

150ml/¼ pint Jersey or full-cream milk

1 heaped tbsp full-fat crème fraîche

30g/1oz unsalted butter

2 organic large eggs

50g/2oz vanilla caster sugar, plus extra to gratinée

120g/4½oz plain flour

Put the prunes into a bowl and sprinkle with the sugar and Cointreau. Leave to soak for 2–3 hours, turning every so often.

Preheat the oven to 180°C/Gas 4. Butter a baking dish well, then dust it with sugar mixed with a little cinnamon if you like, shaking it around until it sticks to the butter.

For the batter, heat the milk and crème fraîche together in a small saucepan to just below the boil, then remove from the heat and add the butter, stirring to melt it.

Beat the eggs and sugar together using an electric mixer until they are pale and have quadrupled in volume, about 5 minutes. Pour in the milk and crème fraîche mixture and fold to combine. Sift in the flour and fold in, whisking out any lumps. The mixture should feel light, frothy and bubbly to the whisk.

Scatter the prunes in the prepared dish and pour over the batter. Bake for 30–40 minutes or until the batter has clearly set at the outside but is still wobbly in the centre.

Heat the grill. Sprinkle the clafoutis liberally with a layer of caster sugar and place under the grill until golden brown.

Serve the clafoutis hot, warm or at room temperature. I like it with crème fraîche flavoured with 1 tbsp of Cointreau and the grated zest of an orange. Plain will do if you prefer.

Fig and raspberry clafoutis

Use 500g/1lb or so figs, cut in half, and the same amount of raspberries. Heat a good knob of butter in a pan and cook the figs for no more than a minute. Toss in the raspberries and sugar, heat for a few seconds until they bleed, then instantly plop them into the prepared gratin dish. Make the batter, pour over the fruit and bake as above. The raspberries will bleed delectably into the batter.

Winter fruit salad

I have long loved bay and citrus. In the winter when Navel oranges arrive – or a little later when blood oranges and Tarocco oranges from Sicily cast their sunset-coloured spell over everything – and there are pomegranates, reminding one of all things bright and exotic, the time comes to make a winter fruit salad that is enough to banish winter blues. This is my current favourite, crimson and green, orange and pink, and not a blue in sight.

serves 6

4 Navel or blood or Tarocco oranges

2 pink grapefruit

12–15 organic Medjool dates (1 box)

1 pomegranate

6 bay leaves

2 heaped tbsp unrefined sugar

a handful of pistachio nuts

As you prepare the citrus fruit, save all the juices, tipping them into the heavy-bottomed pan you are going to make the syrup in. Slice the tops and bottoms off 3 oranges and both grapefruit. Work a sharp knife from the top to the bottom of each, removing the peel and white pith together in strips until you have the naked fruit. Trim off all the pithy bits.

Slice the oranges into circles and throw them into the serving bowl. Cut the grapefruit into segments between the membranes and add them to the bowl. Squeeze the remains of the grapefruit over the pan to extract all the juice. Halve and pit the dates and add them to the citrus fruit.

Extract the juice from the remaining orange and add it to the pan. Similarly, squeeze and add the juice from half of the pomegranate; this is difficult but not impossible. Add the bay leaves and sugar to the pan, bring slowly to the boil to dissolve the sugar and bubble for a few minutes until you have a syrupy consistency.

At this point, throw in the pistachio nuts, cover the pan with a lid and leave to cool until warm. The bay will continue to infuse and scent the syrup.

Disgorge the seeds from the remaining pomegranate half into the fruit salad. Pour the warm syrup over the fruit salad, including the bay, which looks pretty but is there purely for decoration.

Cover the fruit salad and put it in the fridge until just before serving. You may like cream or crème fraîche with it, but I love the purity and flavour on its own. The syrup really is the colour of sunset.

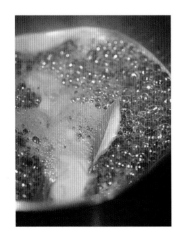

Summer berry gratin

Sometimes in the summer, you get berried out. Particularly if you invite people over at the last minute, you want something a little more special than just a bowl of raspberries or strawberries and cream, or an Eton Mess. The great thing about this gratin is that the fruits are not cooked through, so they retain all their intense, raw flavour. And it is splendiferous to present a dish of them under a scorched top of light-as-air sabayon with billows of cream folded into it. The topping can be made in advance and kept in the fridge until the following day, so play it whichever way suits your hand.

serves 4

300g/10oz strawberries
(a good variety, not the
acidic Elsanta), hulled
300g/10oz raspberries
100g/3½oz blueberries
up to 1 tbsp unrefined
vanilla caster sugar, to taste
1–2 tbsp crème de cassis or
Grand Marnier

for the sabayon

4 organic large egg yolks
120g/4½oz unrefined vanilla
caster sugar
juice of 1 lemon
100ml/3½fl oz Jersey or
double cream

Put the berries into a large bowl and scatter over the sugar and liqueur. Set aside to macerate (see note). After 15 minutes, turn the fruit very gently to encourage the juices to bleed and then leave for a further 10 minutes or so.

To make the sabayon, put the egg yolks, sugar and lemon juice in the top of a double boiler or in a heatproof bowl over a pan of simmering water, making sure the bowl is not touching the water. Whisk, using a hand-held electric whisk, until the mixture has doubled in volume and thickened to the point at which it will leave a trail on top if you lift the beaters. At this point, remove the top pan or bowl to a worktop, setting it down on a folded tea-towel to hold it steady, and continue to whisk until the mixture is cold.

Now whisk the cream to the point at which it has a loose slackness but holds its shape; over-whisking even a little will make it too rigid to incorporate. Fold the cream lightly into the sabayon and either proceed to the finish or, if you are not about to serve the gratin, refrigerate.

Put the macerated fruit into a medium, shallow gratin dish or divide between heatproof, individual, shallow serving bowls. Plop the sabayon evenly over the top.

Heat the grill to its highest setting or get your blow-torch ready. Put the gratin under the grill for about a minute or wave your blow-torch over the surface until it is golden brown. The burnishing has to happen fast so that the sabayon doesn't separate. Serve at once.

If you are preparing the sabayon in advance, macerate the fruit 30 minutes before gratinéeing to serve.

Caramel and cardamom ice cream with Tarocco oranges

Whoever first dreamt up the pairing of oranges and caramel discovered one of those classic combinations that complement and enhance with such simple grace: the sharp tang of citrus, the bittersweet of burnt sugar. This ice cream attains Nirvana when served with either the sharp bite of the red-fleshed winter Tarocco oranges from the slopes beneath Etna, or, if you can't find them, with the sweeter, dark-red flesh of the blood orange. You need not use the cardamom if you want to keep the caramel pure, but a whiff of it does work wonders with an orange.

serves 8

250g/9oz unrefined vanilla caster sugar

1 vanilla pod, cut into a few pieces

350ml/12fl oz Jersey or full-cream milk

8 cardamom pods, gently crushed to open

284ml/10fl oz pot thick Jersey or double cream

8 organic large egg yolks

6 Tarocco or blood oranges

Slowly heat the sugar with the vanilla pod in a wide, heavy-bottomed frying pan without stirring, though if your pan has hot spots you may tilt and swirl it a little, until the sugar has melted completely.

Meanwhile, heat the milk with the cardamom pods to scalding point, then remove from the heat, cover and leave to infuse for 5 minutes.

Once the sugar has melted, let it brown to a dark mahogany all over, at which point you will see darker bubbles beginning to erupt from beneath. Then, and only then, carefully pour over the cream and stir as the two cohere like molten lava. Remove from the heat.

In the meantime, beat the egg yolks in a bowl, strain the infused milk through a sieve onto them and whisk together. Whisk the milk and egg mix into the hot caramel as soon as you take it off the heat. Return the pan to a gentle heat and stir until it is just below boiling point.

Pour into a bowl set in a larger bowl full of ice, or just pour into a bowl and cool more slowly, whatever suits your timing. Once cooled, churn in an ice-cream maker until firm. Or freeze in a plastic container, whisking every 30 minutes to break down the ice crystals.

To prepare the oranges, squeeze the juice from two of them and set aside. Cut away the peel and pith from the rest, in strips from top to bottom. Slice the oranges across into circles and place in a dish. Strain the reserved juice over them, then cover and chill until ready to serve.

You'll only need a few orange slices alongside the untold richness of this most more-ish of ice creams.

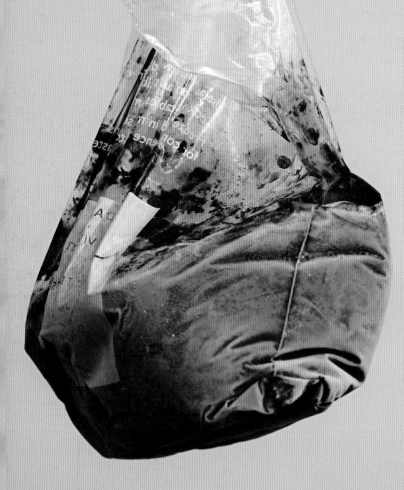

The fruit glut

There's more to this than a bag of frozen fruit. We country mice, with odd recidivist tendencies, are inclined to follow the seasons religiously, disbelieving everything the supermarkets would have us believe about when and how we should buy and eat a peach or cook a salmon. If, like me, you pick, grow and buy from farmers' markets and soft fruit growers, watching for the brief season of each fruit, fowl, fish and vegetable until the price barometer has plummeted and is set fair so you can buy in quantity, then you will know what to do already. You will be doing it.

You'll have pots of scrumminess in your larder or fridge and a freezer full of the joys of spring, summer and autumn – even in the winter. Even so, you may not have thought of everything.

As I write this mid-February, the last of my cooking apple store, somewhat bruised and freckled with brown blotches, is still good enough to bake or purée. And the best way to use up last year's home-made Seville orange marmalade – now a little solid in the pot – is to spoon it over the apples before you bake.

I pick pears to spice and Victoria plums from my trees to freeze; the mulberries and quinces, greengages and walnuts are too young to fruit yet. I risk nature's prickly disdain for man by pulling sloes off their spiky branches in the autumn and gathering damsons and blackberries from tree, orchard and hedgerow.

I make slow, sloe gin – if I can possibly resist dipping into it for a couple of winters the flavour is all the better – likewise the damson. I sozzle blackberries in vodka or freeze them 'au nature' ready for Blackberry and apple Betty (see page 156), pies and crumbles.

I buy kilos of tomatoes from the organic farm down the road to make tomato chilli jam, and for the jars of stove-top dried and slow-roasted tomatoes (see page 161),

which I store and use in the lean, dark months as the year turns.

Blackcurrants and redcurrants and raspberries come from my canes, but if they didn't I would go to a 'pick-your-own'. My store-cupboard mentality of squirrelling and potting the best of a season – to surprise people with when the season's over – is getting more and more, well, squirrelly as the years go by. There's nothing quite like the pleasure of looking at a fully jarred and bottled larder shelf.

As each fruit and vegetable ripens there's a brief plethora, so what I don't eat I freeze, preserve, pickle, chutnefy, turn to jam or jelly, or blitz and sieve raw – ready for a hit of intense blackcurrant vitamin C in a winter sorbet, ice cream or fool. Each time I open the Arctic door and gaze at the purple packets, frosted with rime, it warms the midwinter soul with the comfort of knowing you've got a reminder of summer on a dark, chill night.

The last of the baked apples

I'm not one for the school-dinner golden syrup and currants version. I like to tweak the apple as the year turns. Winter is dried fruit time, so chopped unsulphured apricots pushed down through the core cavity with some sugar and butter and a topknot of my last year's Seville orange marmalade is a possibility. Or some chopped prunes and broken walnuts with apricot jam splodged on top and perhaps a hint of Armagnac or crumbled, almondy amaretti packed inside with the fruit.

Before stuffing, score the apples around their circumference to stop them bursting during baking, prise out the cores almost to the base and brush the skins with melted butter. Sometimes I also roll the apples in light muscovado or demerara sugar flavoured with freshly ground cinnamon and allspice. Stand the apples on a baking tray and fill the cavities generously. Give them 30 minutes in a preheated hottish oven, say 180°C/ Gas 4, until they feel soft right through when tested with a skewer. Serve this easiest and most comforting of puddings with a knob of clotted cream, home-made custard or a good vanilla ice cream.

Stewed Victoria plums

I usually tip my frozen plums straight into an earthenware dish, turn them in sugar – muscovado out of choice for its affinity with the fruit – and add ½ cinnamon stick and 2 tbsp dark rum. That is it.

A kilo/2¼lb of plums to 120g/4oz sugar in my book, since they are an eating plum and anyway I don't like things over-sweetened. Trust to taste, your own – you can always add a little more after cooking but, as they say, you can't take it away.

Cook the plums from frozen, uncovered, in a preheated oven at 150°C/Gas 2 (or in the simmering oven of an Aga) and start checking after 40 minutes. Adjust the sweetness if you need to.

Blackberry and apple brown Betty

This stove-top Betty involves a mere 10 minutes with butter, sugar, fruit and crumbs. And perhaps a little liquor – cassis goes well with this, or a little kirsch. Or if you make this with plums, rum or whiskey is lovely. You can either cook the apples to a purée, which happens anyway with a Bramley or cooker, or slice and fry eating apples in butter as I've done here, adding the blackberries towards the end.

serves 4

for the crumb topping

3–4 slices good stale brown, white or granary bread, crusts removed

60g/2oz unsalted butter

1 tsp freshly ground cinnamon, or more

2 or 3 whole allspice, crushed

1–2 heaped tbsp light muscovado or other sugar

for the fruit

4 good, large, tart apples, such as Egremont Russet or Cox's

30g/1oz unsalted butter

1 tbsp unrefined granulated sugar

a couple of handfuls of blackberries (or raspberries or blackcurrants in season)

1–2 tbsp crème de cassis or kirsch

For the topping, tear the bread to crumbs. Melt the butter in a large frying pan until foaming, then throw in the breadcrumbs and stir to coat them all over. Now stir sporadically over a gentle to medium heat so the crumbs crisp all over, but do not let them turn dark brown. You cannot hurry this.

Meanwhile, peel, core and slice the apples. Cook them with the butter and sugar in another pan, stirring every so often, until softened. Before they collapse, throw in the blackberries and cassis and stir for a few more minutes. (If you use cooking apples, just add more sugar to taste and cook them to a purée before you add the berries.) Once the apples and blackberries are cooked, remove them from the heat.

To finish the topping, add the cinnamon, allspice and muscovado sugar to the crisp crumbs and stir briefly to melt the sugar. Now taste: to get the spicing right you may need up to another 1 tsp cinnamon. Remove from the heat.

Give everybody a generous spoonful or two of fruit and scatter the hot spicy crumb on top. Crème fraîche is good with this.

Blackcurrant sorbet

Raw blackcurrants are like a different fruit entirely to cooked ones, and when it comes to a sorbet or ice cream or fool, there is simply no comparison. That starburst of raw taste smacks tongue and taste buds into total, salivatory submission in an instant. And the slightly musty note in the scent only adds to the little black bauble's naked charms.

I froze bags of raw blackcurrant purée last summer and, astonishingly, its zing factor and colour are barely lessened by 7 months shut away in the cold. The thrill of a blackcurrant out-of-season fool or sorbet is every bit as exciting in winter, when one most craves currants, berries and stone fruit, as it is in the summer when we have them on a plate.

serves 8–10

450g/1lb blackcurrants, stripped of their stems

450ml/¾ pint water

225g/8oz unrefined vanilla caster sugar

a spritz of lemon juice

Do not bother with topping and tailing. Just tip the blackcurrants into the food processor or blender and blitz them to a purple velvet purée. Push through a sieve into a large bowl with a wooden spoon, only discarding the dry, seedy pulp that won't go through. This calls for a little muscle power. (This is the raw purée that I freeze so much of.)

Put the water and sugar in a pan and bring to the boil, then continue to boil for 5 minutes. Cool the sugar syrup in a bowl set in a larger bowl of ice, or just let it cool slowly.

Introduce three-quarters of the sugar syrup to the blackcurrant purée and taste. Remember that all things churned taste sweeter, so at this stage it should be sharp. Add a spritz of lemon juice to accentuate the flavour of the fruit and taste again. You may need to add more of the sugar syrup, you may need another spritz of lemon, it may be perfect. Adjust accordingly.

Churn the mixture in an ice-cream machine until firm. If you do not have one, freeze in a suitable container, whisking every 30 minutes or so to break down the ice crystals.

Either serve the sorbet straight away or keep in a sealed container in the freezer, taking it out about 10 minutes before serving to soften slightly. Like all fruit sorbets, the flavour diminishes quite quickly, so eat within the week. Accompany with little shortbread butter biscuits (see page 53), flavouring them with lavender if it is in season.

Stove-top dried tomatoes

Drying tomatoes like this intensifies the flavour to the most delectable degree and gives you something special to add to a tomato sauce, or use alone. The addition of a few herbs and a little good olive oil gives you the very simplest of pasta sauces. Combine stove-top dried with slow-roasted tomatoes and you have double delicious.

Use the best-flavoured tomatoes you can find – cherry, pomodorino or a larger variety. There is no point in my giving you a quantity, it is up to you entirely. Slice the tomatoes in half and spread them out, cut-side up, on a baking tray. Add a tiny sliver of garlic, a scrunch of salt, a turn of pepper and a few thyme leaves to each and top with a few drops of good olive oil.

I leave mine on the warm plate on top of the Aga, but you can use a warming drawer or a warming oven of a conventional oven. After a few hours when the tomatoes are wrinkling, turn them over. Repeat until the tomatoes are dried but not shrivelled. Mine usually take 24 hours on the Aga; they may take more or less in a conventional warming oven.

Decant to a sterilised screw-top or Kilner jar, pour good olive oil over to cover and seal. Store somewhere cool and not sunlit. Use within 4 months and store in the fridge once opened. The oil is then beautifully flavoured to cook with, or to use again.

Slow-roasted tomatoes

Use full-flavoured, ripe cherry or pomodorino, or plum tomatoes or another larger variety. Pack as many tomatoes as you want to use – tightly but not squeezed together – in a roasting tin or earthenware dish and dribble over a modest few drops of olive oil.

I leave mine in the warming oven of the Aga, but you can use a conventional oven on its lowest possible setting. They will take 3–4 hours. The tomatoes should shrivel up, looking like someone 100 years old, complexion-wise. Check how they are doing every hour until you have the desired cosmetic effect.

When ready, cool to warm and decant into sterilised jars (with sealed tops or screw-tops) and pour over good olive oil to cover. Seal and store somewhere cool and not sunlit. Use within 4 months and store in the fridge once opened.

Tomato chilli jam

I make no apologies for recycling this recipe from my Kitchen Bible, particularly since it is somewhat modified. We obsessive cooks tinker and tweak for amusement, so as not to get stuck in a cooking rut and since we are always in search of that elusive thing, the perfect recipe.

I make batches of this right through the tomato season and give it away, usually over-generously, until I'm left with not enough until the season reappears. I eat it without ever tiring, on Lancashire, Cheddar and single Gloucester, with goat's cheese and Caerphilly, and spooned onto roasted squashes, red onion and sweet potato. I have even been known to deck the odd scallop with it.

makes about 3 jars

1.8kg/4lb very ripe tomatoes

4 medium red chillies, with their seeds

2 hot bonnet chillies, with their seeds

2 green chillies, with their seeds

10 fat garlic cloves, peeled

5 thumbs of fresh root ginger, peeled and roughly chopped

80ml/2½fl oz Thai fish sauce

675g/1½lb unrefined golden caster sugar

200ml/7fl oz red wine vinegar

Chop half of the tomatoes into small dice and set aside. Put the rest of the tomatoes with the chillies and their seeds, garlic, ginger and fish sauce in a blender and blitz to a fine purée.

Spoon the purée into a deep, heavy-bottomed pan and add the sugar and wine vinegar. Bring to the boil slowly, stirring as you go. When it comes to the boil, turn down to a simmer and add the diced tomatoes. Skim off any foam that rises to the surface and cook gently for up to 1½ hours, stirring from time to time, to prevent the mixture catching and burning. Scrape the sides of the pot too, so that everything cooks evenly. The mixture thickens as it cooks – as it reduces and as the pectin in the tomatoes takes effect.

When the mixture seems thick to the stir of a wooden spoon, decant it through a large funnel into warm, sterilised jars and seal.

Store in a larder or cool place, not the fridge, for up to 9 months, though you are unlikely to make it last beyond Christmas. Once opened, keep in the fridge.

Something-out-

I have no idea what's for supper tonight. That's normal for me,
I'm not the sort of person who colour codes their knicker drawer
and works out their menu a month in advance. I like a challenge, a
spur, particularly after shopping and cooking for the weekend. As
I open the fridge door when I stop work tonight, I know there'll be
something to turn into a great supper. Something out of nothing.

It's Monday morning and there are three days left to cook
on-the-hoof before Thursday's farmers' market, a trip to my fish
shop late morning when the boats come in, to the deli and to the
supermarket. This chapter is about working with what you've got
and thinking about shopping and storing so you've always got it.

Consider this. If you can't cook a week's worth of dinners out
of what you have on larder shelf and in store-cupboard, in fridge,
freezer and garden or window box, then something, somewhere is
wrong. Letting your stores run down or shopping daily is a false
economy, both time and money-wise, and leads to despair and
panic buying, to expensive mistakes, to ready-mades and quick-
cooks and a generally less imaginative way of cooking and eating.

Be prepared. For feast rather than famine, that is. It feels so
much better to know that the fridge is stocked with stand-bys,

of-nothing suppers

from tahini and preserved lemons to mustards and a whole rake of different cheeses; with a panoply of half-full condiments or their unopened brethren in the store-cupboard.

Then there are the pulses and pastas, polentas and rices, oils and vinegars; I won't go on. Common sense in the kitchen is not so common these days – the persuasive powers of the supermarket would lead us into temptation down every aisle, but be bold and resolute, stick to the stove, learn to love your leftovers and cook when there's nothing in the house.

If the horrifying statistic that we throw away 30% of the food we buy is true, we can live better for less if we only incorporate yesterday's leftovers into tonight's supper. When I throw a lemon risotto at my children, or home-made baked beans, or a tart made with leek tops and the ends of an old goat – as in crottin – they are as content as they would be with a hunk of meat and two veg.

I always try to have a lump of fresh yeast for a pizza or bread; it really isn't any trouble to make either. And the store-cupboard is a treasure trove to plunder for a pizza – made with a little leftover tomato sauce, my favourite charcoal-grilled artichokes, roasted peppers (also from a jar), good olives or black olive paste from Seggiano, baby capers, mozzarella and salami.

A chick pea curry that my daughter Charissa learned last year, while working in an orphanage in the Himalayas, has entered the repertoire as a staple. Once the roles have been reversed and your children start cooking for you, you have another pleasure in store, not just their food and a night off, but a chance to encourage and teach them how to make something out of nothing so that they, too, are equipped not just for student life, but for life.

Chick pea masala

When my younger daughter Charissa went to work in an orphanage in the foothills of the Himalayas last year, all the food was grown on the nearby family farm. She learned to cook with Mrs Khani, who ran the place with her husband and prepared everything every day from scratch, from the chapattis to the wonderful vegetarian dishes indigenous to the region. Charissa came back with all the recipes in a little booklet. Here are the ones we love best.

Serve them all together with spiced basmati rice and your favourite curry accompaniments: raita, sliced banana sprinkled with fried onion seeds and crushed cardamom, and a good mango chutney won't go amiss.

serves 4

300g/10oz dried chick peas, soaked in cold water for at least 8 hours

2 tbsp olive oil

1 onion, peeled and sliced

¼ tsp ground turmeric

1 tsp chilli powder

½ tsp ground coriander

1 tsp sea salt

1 tbsp ginger and garlic paste (fresh ginger and garlic pounded together)

4 large tomatoes, chopped

½ tsp garam masala

a handful of coriander leaves, chopped

Drain the soaked chick peas and tip them into a saucepan. Add enough water to cover by about 2cm/¾ inch, but don't add salt at this stage. Bring to the boil, cover and lower the heat. Simmer for 1½–2 hours until tender.

Heat the olive oil in a frying pan over a medium heat, then add the onion and cook until golden and softened.

Meanwhile, in a blender or food processor, whiz the turmeric, chilli powder, ground coriander, salt, garlic and ginger paste and one of the chopped tomatoes with a little water to form a paste.

Add this masala paste to the onion and cook over a medium heat for 5–10 minutes until the colour darkens and the oil comes to the surface. Stir in the chick peas, then cover and simmer gently for 15 minutes.

Add the rest of the tomatoes, garam masala and chopped coriander and heat for a few minutes.

Aloo palak (Spiced potato and spinach)

serves 4

2 tbsp olive oil

2 garlic cloves, peeled and sliced

2 green chillies, sliced

1 tsp ground turmeric

sea salt

500g/1lb 2oz spinach, washed and chopped

2 medium potatoes, peeled and cubed

2 tomatoes, chopped

Heat the olive oil in a wok or frying pan over a medium heat. When hot, add the sliced garlic and cook until it just begins to colour, then add the chillies with their seeds. Cook for about 5 minutes until the chillies start to darken, then sprinkle over the turmeric and salt and cook for a few seconds.

Add the chopped spinach and cubed potatoes, mix well and cook for 2 minutes. Stir in the chopped tomatoes, then cover and cook for 20 minutes or until the potatoes are tender.

Mint chutney

If you do not have any tamarind paste in your store-cupboard, you can make a simple fresh chutney by blitzing the mint leaves with a little lemon juice and adjusting to taste.

serves 4

50g/2oz mint leaves
50g/2oz coriander leaves
3 garlic cloves, peeled
3 green chillies
1 tsp sea salt
2 tbsp tamarind juice
½ tsp toasted cumin seeds

Whiz everything together in a blender, then taste and adjust the seasoning if you need to. Scrape into a serving bowl.

For the tamarind juice, you will need to soak 1 tbsp tamarind paste in 2 tbsp boiling water for about 10 minutes, then strain to remove the seeds. Toast the cumin seeds briefly in a hot, dry pan until they just change colour, about 30 seconds.

Red onion squash gnocchi
with sage butter

Whenever I make gnocchi I wonder why I don't make them more often. They are deceptively easy to get right and make you feel proud each time they rise magically in the simmering water. And they turn out as light as a cloud, yet as substantial as you could wish for.

These little pillows of cheesy, nutmeggy squash are dressed with salty, sharp pecorino and Parmesan and coated in glossy butter with lovely fusty fried sage leaves. A radicchio salad with some watercress and a little Gem lettuce, dressed with best balsamic and olive oil, is the only accompaniment you'll need.

serves 2

a little olive oil

1 red onion squash, about 250g/9oz

100–120g/3½–4½oz '00' Italian flour

1 tsp baking powder

sea salt and black pepper

1 organic large egg

4 tbsp freshly grated aged Parmigiano-Reggiano

nutmeg for grating

12 young, soft sage leaves

30–45g/1–1½oz unsalted butter, plus an extra knob to serve if you like

2 tbsp freshly grated pecorino, or extra Parmesan if that's all you have

Preheat the oven to 200°C/Gas 6. Halve the squash and scoop out the seeds with a spoon, then plonk both halves, cut side down, on a lightly oiled baking tray. Roast for 45 minutes or until tender when pierced through with a skewer. Lower the oven setting to 150°C/Gas 2.

Scoop out the cooked pulp and push it through the coarse disc of a mouli or through a potato ricer into a large bowl. If it seems wet, dry it out by stirring it in a pan over a medium heat for a few minutes, then place in the bowl.

Sift in 100g/3½oz of the flour with the baking powder and 1 tsp salt and break the egg into the mixture. Mix well and add 2 tbsp Parmesan and a grating of nutmeg – slightly more than the usual restrained grating. The mixture will be tacky and sticky, so it will stick to your hands, but only add more flour if it seems runnier rather than gloopy.

Bring a large, heavy-bottomed pan of salted water to the boil. Meanwhile, with floured hands, shape the dough into small dessertspoonfuls. Dunk them in a little more flour to coat all over, shaking off the excess, and plop them onto a large plate.

Roll up the sage leaves together and slice finely to cut them into long, thin shreds. Melt the butter in a pan, add the sage and heat until it turns crisp, not letting the butter brown.

Warm a large, greased gratin dish in the oven. Drop half of the gnocchi into the boiling water with a spoon, spacing them apart, and keep the water at a gentle simmer. The gnocchi will take longer than you think to start rising to the surface but they will, and when they do, allow them another 3 minutes, then scoop them out with a slotted spoon and plop them into the gratin dish with a little of their cooking water to keep them moist. You can pour over the sage butter and sprinkle with a little of the remaining Parmesan and pecorino at this stage too. Pop them into the oven to keep warm.

Cook the second lot of gnocchi and then add them to the gratin dish. Sprinkle with more cheese and serve on warmed plates with the rest of the cheese in a bowl alongside. Scrunch pepper over the gnocchi and top with a little knob of butter if you feel like it before you bring the dish to the table.

Spanish tortilla

The classic Spanish tortilla is a simple egg, potato and olive oil affair, but I usually add to it with a red and green layer of roasted peppers and wilted spinach, and often a tangle of softened onions too. Unlike a normal omelette, a tortilla will keep for a couple of days. You can eat it hot, warm or cold, or reheat it in some Romesco or tomato sauce. One of the best dishes to take on a picnic.

serves 4

about 500g/1lb 2oz potatoes, peeled
sea salt and black pepper
3–4 tbsp good fruity olive oil
6 organic large eggs

flavourings (optional)

2 large onions, peeled and finely sliced
a little olive oil
2 red peppers, charred or roasted and skinned, cored and deseeded, or a handful of piquillo peppers from a jar
500g/1lb 2oz spinach, washed

to serve (optional)

Romesco (see page 113), puréed rather than coarse-textured, or any home-made tomato sauce (see page 174)

Add the potatoes to a pan of salted water and parboil for 10 minutes or so until almost al dente. Drain and cut into small cubes when cool enough to handle. Choose a frying pan that is deep rather than wide, and oil the bottom and sides. Add 2–3 tbsp olive oil and place over a moderate heat. When hot, add the cubed potatoes and cook gently on all sides until tender, but don't allow them to colour.

In the meantime, prepare the flavourings, if using. Cook the onions in a little olive oil until very soft. Cut the peppers into strips. Cook the spinach in a pan with just the water clinging to the leaves after washing until it just collapses, then tip into a sieve and press with the back of a spoon to remove the water.

Beat the eggs in a bowl and season them. Cover the potatoes with the onion slices and strips of red pepper, then strew the spinach over the surface, if using. Pour in the beaten eggs and cook over a high heat for a minute, then turn the heat down and let the tortilla cook slowly, right through. Shake the pan a little to make sure it doesn't stick.

When you see that the top of the egg is no longer liquid, even in the middle, cover the pan with a large, flat plate and invert the tortilla onto it. Add another 1 tbsp of olive oil to the pan, slide the tortilla back in and cook for another minute or two.

Slide the finished tortilla out onto a large, warmed plate. Serve as it is, or with some well puréed Romesco or tomato sauce.

If flipping the tortilla is too daunting, once the top is set put the pan under the grill for a few minutes and let the tortilla brown and puff up a little.

Paella with spring vegetables

serves 6

450g/1lb mussels or carpet shell clams, or both, plus 450g/1lb monkfish fillet, cubed

4 tbsp olive oil

1 large onion, peeled and chopped

180g/6oz unsmoked streaky bacon or pancetta, snipped into small strips

2 garlic cloves, peeled and finely chopped

6 baby carrots

850ml1⅓ pints chicken stock

150ml/¼ pint dry white wine

450g/1lb Calasparra rice

a small bunch of flat-leaf parsley, leaves chopped

large pinch of saffron stamens

6 asparagus spears, woody ends snapped off, cut into short lengths

100g/3½oz shelled baby broad beans (blanched and skinned if any larger)

100g/3½oz shelled fresh peas

6 baby courgettes, cut in half

2 large tomatoes, skinned, deseeded and chopped

sea salt and black pepper

They may be called spring vegetables, but in these cold climes they are mostly available in the early summer. Asparagus is the first to arrive with its short 6-week season in late spring.

You can change the ingredients as they come and go, from artichokes to mangetout, baby courgettes to young carrots and turnips, remembering that all paellas traditionally incorporate some part of a pig. So unless you don't eat pig, a little pancetta or bacon works beautifully here with the shellfish and spring veg. Or if you have some chorizo sitting in the fridge, use it instead and you'll find it colours the dish a lovely brick red.

I like to use the traditional Spanish Calasparra rice for a paella, but Italian risotto rice is an option if that's what you have in your store-cupboard. As for timing, the rice takes around 25 minutes to cook.

Scrub the mussels and clams thoroughly in cold water, removing the beards from the mussels and discarding any with open shells that do not close when sharply tapped. Set aside in a bowl of cold, salted water.

Heat the olive oil in a paella pan or large, heavy-bottomed frying pan, then add the onion and bacon and fry over a moderate heat until the onion begins to soften. Add the garlic and carrots and turn to coat in the oil for a few minutes. Meanwhile, bring the stock and wine to the boil in another pan and lower the heat to a simmer; keep it like this throughout the cooking process.

Add the rice and half the parsley to the paella pan and stir to coat in the oil. Then add about a quarter of the stock and wine, throw in your saffron and stir it in. As soon as the liquid has been absorbed by the rice, pour in another quarter, adding the asparagus at this stage. When this has been absorbed, add the third quarter along with the broad beans and peas.

Add the courgettes with the last lot of the stock and wine and throw in the chopped tomatoes and shellfish, along with the monkfish if using. Cover the pan now, just until the shellfish have opened, which will only take a few minutes. Season, then taste and adjust. Once the rice is cooked, take the pan off the heat and leave the paella, covered, for 5 minutes to allow the flavours to marry.

Remove the lid, sprinkle over the rest of the chopped parsley and serve straight from the pan.

Grilled sardines or mackerel
with green and black olive salsa

Fresh sardines, like fresh mackerel, are hard to come by in England. Both are the sort of oily fish that need to be eaten on the day they were pulled from the deep. I do this with mackerel in the summer in the west of Ireland because I pull them out of the deep myself, or my neighbours come round with a rake of them they've gone out and caught. However, with sardines, I tend to opt for frozen ones if I see them – Portuguese sardines are frozen the moment they hit the deck and are nearly as good as the fresh. I buy them by the bag for pasta con le sarde – a lovely baked pasta, fennel and sardine dish flavoured with anchovies, raisins and pine nuts – and for this lovely Provençal-inspired dish.

serves 4

5–6 sardines (or 1 mackerel)
per person
olive oil for brushing
sea salt and black pepper

for the olive salsa

about 4 tbsp good, peppery
olive oil
6 large green olives, pitted
and sliced
8–10 smaller Taggiasca or
Nyons olives, halved and
pitted
24 cherry tomatoes, halved
a handful of basil leaves,
chopped
grated zest and juice of
1 organic lemon

to serve

tomato balsamico (see page
174), warm

Make the olive salsa about 30 minutes ahead so that the flavours get a chance to mingle. Pour the olive oil into a bowl and throw in the olives together with the tomatoes, chopped basil and lemon zest and juice. Toss all together and repeat just before you use it.

Meanwhile, scrape the scales from the sardines with a knife over the sink. You must do this thoroughly before rinsing the fish under cold water and feeling for any stray scales with your fingers. Behead and gut the fish, unless your fishmonger has done it for you, by cutting a small slit from just below the head on the underside of each fish to the belly, where it swells, and removing the innards. Wash again, under cold water. Press the central backbone right down its length and remove it. (If you are using mackerel, fillet the fish, cutting either side of the spine to release the two fillets.) Check over the fish for any small bones.

Place the sardines on a baking tray, skin-side up, and brush them all with a little olive oil. Season and place under a hot grill for about 5 minutes until bubbling and the skin has started to blacken and blister in patches. (If you are cooking mackerel, just keep them under the grill for about another 5 minutes, skin-side up throughout.) The magical, oily juices that collect in the bottom of the tray are to be poured back over the fish, not thrown away.

Place a good spoonful of warm tomato balsamico on each warmed plate and lay the grilled sardines (or mackerel) on top. Spoon some of the olive salsa onto the side of each plate and serve the rest separately in a bowl. Alternatively, present the whole lot on a large platter.

Tomato balsamico

Tomato is possibly the most versatile sauce in the world. It works with chunks of white fish, with meatballs and meatloaf, with stuffed vegetables, and with pasta and a host of other store-cupboard items for easy suppers (see right). This is really just a jazzed-up version of an everyday tomato sauce, easily assembled from ingredients you are likely to have to hand.

serves 4

3 tbsp olive oil

1 onion, peeled and finely chopped

3 garlic cloves, peeled and finely chopped

400g/14oz tin cherry tomatoes

1 tbsp tomato purée

2 tbsp good aged balsamic vinegar

a long strip of orange zest from an organic orange

sea salt and black pepper

Heat the olive oil in a pan over a medium heat until hot, then throw in the onion and garlic and cook until softened and pale golden, about 10 minutes.

Add the tin of tomatoes, tomato purée, balsamic vinegar, orange zest and some seasoning. Bring to a simmer and bubble at a burble, nothing too fast and furious, until the liquid has mostly evaporated from around the tomatoes but they are still whole, about 10–15 minutes. Taste and adjust the seasoning if you need to.

Tomato sauce with carrot, basil and cream

Any riff on a tomato sauce is worth adding to your repertoire. And this one gives you the option of using fresh or tinned plum tomatoes. It freezes well with either, though I normally never get it as far as the freezer. I cook it one night and leave it in the fridge to turn into something else the next day or later in the week.

serves 6

1.5kg/3¼lb fresh ripe tomatoes in season, or 3 x 400g/14oz tins plum tomatoes

85g/3oz unsalted butter

6 tbsp very finely diced carrots

1 medium onion, peeled and very finely chopped

2 celery stalks, de-strung with a potato peeler and very finely chopped

sea salt and black pepper

1 tbsp olive oil (if using tinned tomatoes)

150ml/¼ pint double cream

a handful of basil leaves

If using fresh tomatoes, cut in half vertically and put them in a heavy-bottomed pan over a medium heat. As they begin to cook, put the lid on and turn the heat down a little. Cook gently for 10 minutes, then push the tomatoes through the coarse disc of a mouli. Return to the pan and add the rest of the ingredients, except the cream and half the basil. Cook, uncovered, at a mere blip for 45–60 minutes, giving the pan an occasional stir to stop anything from sticking.

If you are using tinned tomatoes, start the carrots, onion and celery off in a little olive oil to soften them a bit. Meanwhile, put the tinned tomatoes straight through the mouli and then add them to the pan. Cook as above.

Add the cream, turn the heat up a little and stir at a bubble for a minute or two. Remove from the heat, check the seasoning and tear in the rest of the basil leaves.

Tomato sauce with store-cupboard additives

The tomato balsamico and tomato, carrot and basil cream sauce, opposite, both lend themselves to a variety of store-cupboard suppers if you have the right ingredients to hand.

Sometimes you want a sauce as coarse as nature intended it for a simple pasta dish or to douse some home-made mozzarella meatballs. At other times you want a slightly smoother texture, best achieved by putting the sauce through the coarse blade of the mouli. This is the texture I prefer for a pizza topping.

Sometimes you will want to pep up your tomato sauce with a few chilli flakes or shakes of Tabasco to make an arrabiatta pasta sauce. Or you will add black olives, chillies, anchovies, capers, and perhaps a little black olive paste, for a puttanesca. Crumbled tuna also works well in a basic tomato sauce, the ventresca or belly for preference.

For the pasta dish below, I used some leftover filling from the autumn lasagne (on page 70),

tossing in a few spoonfuls of leftover tomato sauce along with some stove-top dried tomatoes and a handful of slow-roasted tomatoes (see page 161) from the store-cupboard.

If your cupboard possesses a bag of the lovely Il Saraceno polenta, a puttanesca is great made with polenta instead of pasta, with some Parmesan and butter stirred into it. You can drape a branch or two of roasted vine tomatoes on top of the sauce on each plate too, to spruce it up. Or add a sliced, roasted aubergine to the tomato sauce; simply brush the aubergine with oil and roast on a baking tray in the oven at 200°C/Gas 6 for 15 minutes first.

There really is no end to the charm of a tomato sauce, and it is worth always keeping your options open by having all the aforementioned ingredients in your cupboard – like a kind of culinary Band-aid – for all eventualities, for a something-out-of-nothing night.

Salade niçoise

The great thing about this vibrant, techni-coloured dream of a many layered dish is that you just put in whatever you have in the summer season, whatever is at its best. And you can choose to include cooked, charcoal-grilled or raw ingredients, depending on your store-cupboard and your time. Any leftovers can go into my favourite summer sandwich the next day, the mighty Pan bagna (see overleaf).

serves 6

4 large tomatoes

225g/8oz green beans, topped and tailed

sea salt and black pepper

⅓ cucumber

1 red pepper

1 yellow pepper

1 large garlic clove, peeled and crushed

juice of 1½–2 lemons

6 tbsp good olive oil

1 little Gem lettuce, washed

a small handful of basil leaves

a few sprigs of parsley

6 chargrilled artichoke hearts (Seggiano are the best), or cooked baby artichokes

a bunch of spring onions, trimmed and sliced

6 large radishes, halved, a little green top left on

6 organic large eggs

160–200g/6–7oz tin good-quality tuna (ideally ventresca), in olive oil

a large handful of olives, preferably Nyons, pitted

12 good-quality anchovy fillets, rinsed and drained

Core the tomatoes and cut them into quarters, or chop them further if they are the enormous Provençal ones.

Throw the green beans into a pan of boiling, salted water and cook until just softer than al dente, then immediately drain and refresh under cold water to retain their colour and crunch. Peel the cucumber, halve lengthways and scoop out the seeds, then cut into batons.

Hold the peppers over a flame with a pair of tongs or grill them until scorched and charred all over, then put into a bowl and cover with cling film to encourage the steam to lift the skins. When cool enough to handle, peel the peppers and remove the core and seeds, then slice them into strips.

For the dressing, put the garlic in the salad serving bowl and pour over the lemon juice and olive oil. Season with salt and pepper. Whisk using a small whisk or fork and taste and adjust the seasoning.

Tear the lettuce, basil and parsley leaves into the salad bowl. Add the tomatoes, beans, cucumber, peppers, cooked baby artichokes if using, spring onions and radishes and toss together very gently. Leave to stand for 30 minutes to an hour.

In the meantime, boil the eggs for 6–7 minutes, depending on size, so they are the soft side of hard-boiled. Drain and cool under cold water, then peel and halve.

Toss the salad in the bowl, again gently, then crumble in the tuna and add the olives and artichokes if they are chargrilled from a jar. Add the halved eggs, anchovies and a little more olive oil. Scrunch over a little pepper and a sprinkling of salt, but go easy as anchovies are salty.

Pan bagna

You may engineer leftovers of the Salade niçoise on the previous page by making it for fewer people, or by upping the quantities.

Split a fresh baguette or ciabatta in half horizontally and scoop out some of the crumb, not all, with your fingers from the lower side of the loaf. Rub the cut sides with garlic and sprinkle over a tiny bit of red wine vinegar or tarragon vinegar.

Pile the niçoise filling into the excavated side, sprinkle with more olive oil, seasoning and chopped basil. Oil the cut surface of the top half before closing it down onto the pile of goodies. Wrap in foil and weight down overnight in the fridge.

The following day, allow the pan bagna to come back to room temperature out of the foil before eating. Perfect picnic food.

Leek and potato cake
with black pudding and cheese

A paupery of ingredients in vegetable rack and fridge, but a wonder of a simple, comforting supper is lurking there. Half a black pudding left over from the Stuffed pork fillet with figs and Marsala (see page 143) inspired this recipe. Bubbling with good cheese and richly flavoured with leeks and black pud, this potato cake needs nothing else, unless you feel like a green Cos salad on the side.

serves 2

450g/1lb potatoes, peeled
sea salt and black pepper
1 tbsp olive oil
a few knobs of butter
2 leeks, washed and both green and white chopped
½ black pudding
a little milk
about 30g/1oz Beenleigh Blue, or similar cheese
about 30g/1oz Comté, Gruyère or similar cheese
1 tbsp freshly grated Parmesan

Preheat the oven to 190°C/Gas 5. Boil the potatoes in salted water in the usual way. In the meantime, heat the olive oil and a knob of butter in a pan and sauté the chopped leeks until softened. Crumble in the black pudding and fry, stirring, for a few minutes.

When the potatoes are cooked, drain and mash them with a couple of knobs of butter and a little milk. Tip half of the mash into a small-medium, heavy-bottomed frying pan with an ovenproof handle and flatten. Pile the leek and black pud mixture on top.

Crumble the blue cheese over the surface and top with the grated Comté. Cover with the rest of the mash, flatten and sprinkle with the Parmesan and a scrunch of pepper. Bake for 25 minutes until bubbling, oozing and golden.

Supper, for a song, in a pan.

Boston baked borlotti beans

Deep flavours, deep and dark; sticky, intense and as savoury and piquant and mellow as you could wish for, this is the best version of the dish I have come up with. My take has blackstrap molasses and molasses sugar, runny honey, tamari, tomato and mustard, along with star anise. Classically, this dish is made with ham hocks, so you might like to add some pancetta or lardons, fried until the fat begins to run, or just keep it veggie. Borlotti beans retain their shape and texture well, so they are ideal for this dish.

Start the day before, as you need to soak the beans first, or soak them in the morning and get cracking in the early afternoon.

Perfect with sausages and mash, or just mash.

serves 4

225g/8oz borlotti beans or black-eyed peas, soaked in cold water for at least 8 hours

a sprig of rosemary

2 bay leaves

1 onion, peeled and stuck with 2 cloves

400g/14oz tin cherry tomatoes

1 heaped tbsp blackstrap molasses

1 tbsp runny honey

1 level tbsp molasses sugar

1 level tbsp grain mustard

1 tbsp tamari sauce

a few shakes of Tabasco

1 star anise

5 white peppercorns

8–10 thin slivers of lardo (optional)

Drain the beans and put them into a medium-small, cast-iron cooking pot or similar pan and add the rosemary, bay leaves and onion stuck with cloves. Just cover with cold water and bring to the boil, then reduce to a simmer and put the lid on. Put into a low oven at 140°C/Gas 1 or continue to simmer gently on top of the stove for an hour.

Drain the beans and return them to the cooking pot, keeping their water to use for a soup; discard the herbs. Add the tomatoes to the beans. Thin the molasses with 2 tbsp of the saved hot cooking water and add to the beans with the runny honey and molasses sugar. Stir these together a little and then add the mustard, tamari, Tabasco, star anise and white peppercorns.

Bring just to the boil again, then cover and continue to cook in the oven or slowly on the hob for another hour.

Now remove the lid and turn the oven up to 180°C/Gas 4. The liquid will still be thin at this point. If using lardo, lay the slivers on top of the beans. Continue to cook for up to 3 hours, without a lid, until the liquid has turned into a thick, black, sticky gooey sauce. You may give the dish a gentle stir once or twice to amalgamate everything as it thickens and darkens. The depth of flavour is sensational.

Baked beans with a green herb and Parmesan crust

Instead of borlotti beans, soak the same quantity of haricot or flageolet beans and cook as above until tender, about an hour. Drain, keeping back a few tbsp of cooking liquor, then turn them in 3 ladlefuls of home-made tomato sauce (see page 174), which may be coarse textured or roughly puréed.

Either use 4 tbsp Provençal breadcrumbs (see page 114) or whiz the chopped leaves from a large bunch of flat-leaf parsley with some plain dried crumbs to make the crust green. Sprinkle 2 tbsp Parmesan into the crumb mixture, then scatter it on top of the beans. Dot with butter and bake at 180°C/Gas 4 for about 20–25 minutes. Eat with or without sausages and a jacket potato if you like.

Baked penne with aubergine and tomatoes

A simple, lustrous peasant dish from Puglia that has the satisfaction principle at heart.
I don't see any need to salt the aubergines before roasting.

serves 6

2 large aubergines, cubed into small dice

olive oil to dribble

sea salt and black pepper

450–500g/1lb–1lb 2oz penne or similar pasta

small knob of butter, the size of a walnut

3 ladlefuls, about 375ml/ 12fl oz any home-made tomato sauce (see page 174)

675g/1½lb good tomatoes, sliced

90g/3oz breadcrumbs

90g/3oz Parmesan or pecorino, or a mixture

a few sprigs of basil, leaves torn

Preheat the oven to 180°C/Gas 4. Throw the aubergine cubes into a bowl and dribble over enough olive oil to coat them. Season and toss well, then scatter the cubes on a baking sheet and bake for 15 minutes, or until they feel tender when tested with a skewer.

In the meantime, bring a large pan of salted water to the boil. Add the pasta and cook to the slightly firmer side of al dente. Drain, holding back a few tbsp of the cooking water. Return it to the pan with the reserved water and add the knob of butter. Fold in half of the tomato sauce at this point.

Lay half of the tomato slices over the base of an oiled gratin dish. Sprinkle half the breadcrumbs over the top and season. Layer half the tomatoey pasta on top, followed by half the cubed aubergines.

Spread a quarter of the remaining tomato sauce on top, then sprinkle over half the grated cheese and half the torn basil. Now add the remaining pasta, then the rest of the aubergines and tomato sauce.

Scatter over the rest of the cheese and the basil and add the final layer of tomatoes. Sprinkle with the remaining breadcrumbs and dribble over some extra olive oil. Bake for 45 minutes to 1 hour. The dish should be deliciously crusted, bubbling and brown on top.

Leave to stand for 10–15 minutes before serving. The flavours develop and intensify as the dish begins to cool.

Pasta con la Mollica

Simply pasta with breadcrumbs, tomatoes, parsley and anchovies, this is most definitely a store-cupboard supper. I have started using the tins of organic cherry tomatoes that have appeared recently to make this kind of dish, as they keep their shape and have a good flavour. It is important to use crunchy breadcrumbs, made from stale, good, crustless bread, toasted in a warm oven on a baking tray until crisp.

serves 4

4–6 tbsp olive oil

2 garlic cloves, peeled and thinly sliced

1 celery stalk, de-strung with a potato peeler and finely chopped

1 dried kashmiri chilli, crumbled, or 1 tsp dried chilli flakes

2 tbsp chopped flat-leaf parsley

400g/14oz tin cherry tomatoes

450g/1lb spaghetti or linguine

sea salt and black pepper

8 anchovies, chopped

1 tsp dried oregano

2 tbsp green olives, pitted and sliced

4 heaped tbsp good dried breadcrumbs

knob of butter (optional)

Heat 2 tbsp olive oil in a large, heavy-bottomed frying pan and add the garlic, celery, crumbled chilli and parsley. Sauté over a medium heat for a couple of minutes, then throw in the tomatoes and cook more briskly, stirring, for 10 minutes.

Meanwhile, add the pasta to a pan of boiling, salted water and cook until al dente.

Add the chopped anchovies, oregano and olives to the tomato mixture and cook for a further few minutes. Drain the pasta when it is ready and slip it into the frying pan, stirring to mix everything together.

Add the toasted breadcrumbs and continue to cook for another minute. Taste for seasoning. Add more oil if the dish needs it and, if you like, a knob of butter. I always add butter, even to an olive oil based pasta sauce.

Pizza

Pizza is not just a dish, it is an activity, a family thing, a start of the weekend, Friday night thing that is so much easier than it seems and so much more satisfying. Everyone joins in, even if only to choose the bits and pieces to anoint the great, flat slipper with, and if you want to fold it over calzone-style, the Italian answer to a pasty, well just go for it. This is fun cooking with the sort of ingredients I've always got to hand.

makes two large pizzas

for the pizza dough

500g/1lb 2oz strong white bread flour

7g/¼oz sachet fast-action dry yeast

2 tsp sea salt

1 tbsp olive oil

about 350ml/12fl oz nearly hot water (between hot and tepid)

semolina flour, for dusting

for the toppings

home-made tomato sauce of any kind (see page 174), preferably coarse-textured rather than smooth

plus any of the following:

a 400g/14oz mozzarella di bufala campana, torn into chunks

1–2 garlic cloves, peeled and cut into slivers

cooked crimini or chestnut mushrooms

flamed or grilled red peppers, skinned and sliced into strips

chargrilled artichoke hearts, from a jar

cubed aubergine, roasted in olive oil

salami or prosciutto slices

green and black olives

tiny capers, rinsed and drained

good-quality anchovies

fresh coarsely grated Parmesan

olive oil, preferably herb-flavoured, for brushing

a few basil leaves, shredded or torn

a glug of extra virgin olive oil

To make the dough, tip the flour straight onto your work surface, like all self-respecting Italians do, and add the yeast and salt. Make a well in the middle and pour in the olive oil followed by about two-thirds of the warm water. Begin to knead by tipping the inside wall of flour into the middle and gathering flour as you go. When it gets difficult to knead, add more warm water. Continue until you have a dough.

Turn the dough onto a lightly floured surface and knead for about 10 minutes, stretching it away from you with the heel of your hand every so often, then furling it back towards you with your fingers. Divide in two, shape into balls and place on an oiled baking sheet. Cover with a plastic bag and leave to rise in a warm place until they have doubled in size, about 1½ hours.

Preheat the oven to its highest setting, at least 230°C/Gas 8. Scatter semolina flour over 2 baking trays. Working with one ball at a time, knock down the dough, stretch it and then roll it out until about 5mm/¼ inch thick. Don't worry, it will shrink and spring back to begin with but eventually it will obey your command. Keep the rim a little thicker. Repeat with the other ball of dough.

Spread your tomato sauce generously over the dough with a palette knife, to the rim. Now add your choice of toppings, any combination you like. If you divide the pizza into four windows and fill each one with a different topping, you have a work of art!

Bake the pizzas for 15 minutes before checking. The edges should be brown. Remove from the oven and brush the rim instantly with a little herb-flavoured olive oil. A scattering of basil and a dribble of olive oil on top of the pizza and it is ready.

Leftover ratatouille is a good alternative to the tomato sauce topping. Just add olive oil, garlic slivers, thyme or oregano, sea salt and pepper and a few dried chilli flakes. If you have stove-top dried or slow-roasted tomatoes (see page 161) to hand, throw some in too.

For a simple topping, when good tomatoes are around in the summer, blanch and skin 500g/1lb or so, then chop, discarding the seeds and juice. Cover the pizza dough with the chopped tomatoes, then add oregano, garlic and olive oil. Simple and sumptuous.

Index

Publishing director Jane O'Shea
Creative director Helen Lewis
Project editor Janet Illsley
Art direction & design Lawrence Morton
Photographer James Merrell
Stylist Cynthia Irons
Production director Vincent Smith
Production controller Aysun Hughes

First published in 2009 by
Quadrille Publishing Limited
Alhambra House
27–31 Charing Cross Road
London WC2H 0LS
www.quadrille.co.uk

Text © 2009 Tamasin Day-Lewis
Photography © 2009 James Merrell
Design and layout © 2009 Quadrille
Publishing Limited

Cataloguing in Publication Data: a catalogue
record for this book is available from the
British Library.

ISBN 978 184400 743 1

Printed in China

For P, a lifetime of
friendship, music and
good dinners is not to
be underestimated.
This book is for you
in celebration of this
year's big event.

Songs of Praise for the *Supper for a Song* team

Jane O'Shea for taking the idea and running with it
from start to finish.

Janet Illsley for total attention to detail, no note too
small to escape her notice.

Lawrence Morton whose inspired art direction has
made it a book of beauty and wit.

James Merrell who has a painter's eye, and has married
still-life to composition, process to finished dish.

Patricia Stone, a source of calm, fun and occasional
hysteria – every kitchen needs all three – as she helped
cook the book for the photographs.

Edward Latter who helped cook on one of the shoots
and will surely go far.

Alison Cathie for inviting me to dance at Quadrille.